your lucky stars

what the stars say

about your

luck

every hour
every day
all year long

BY

alexander h. khalil-elyott

winicorp

p.o. box 3314

san leandro ca 94578

YOUR LUCKY STARS

What the Stars Say About Your Luck
Every Hour - Every Day-
All Year Long

Copyright © Alexander H. Khalil-Ellyott

First Printing 1983

Printed in the United States of America

Library of Congress Cataloging in
Publication Data

Khalil-Elyott, Alexander H., 1921-
     Your Lucky Stars

     1. Astrology.   2. Gambling--
Miscellanea. I. Title.
BF1729.G3K42 1983 133.5'8795 83-50381
ISBN 0-9610634-2-4

Paperback

DEDICATION

For Winnie,
keeper of the
faith.

PUBLISHER

**WINICORP
BOX 3314
SAN LEANDRO
CA 94578**

AUTHOR'S FOREWORD
ALEXANDER H. KHALIL-ELYOTT

During World War II nothing happened. Seldom does in non-combat zones. After demob went back to the University where also nothing happened. Joined the family business; small manufacturers in London, and again nothing happened.

A year after entering business, married a lady from the north of England. She belongs to one of those ancient families called farmers but whose entire lives revolve around horses. Over the years, had three children and uncounted horses. The horses were my wife, Maeve's, special interest. I simply didn't have the time to participate in breeding, training, handling, showing, racing, sales and all the other things one must do with horses.

Things had started to happen and did so with increasing frequency and speed. The little company I'd joined, through acquisitions, trades purchases, mergers, exchanges of stock, etc., had grown to be among the very largest British-Canadian-American conglomerates. One day's world-wide business is now more than four times the yearly sales of the original company. Have held several increasingly important jobs until I reached my present position, Vice-President, Purchasing.

A funny thing happened to me on the way to retirement. A wave of computer based technology washed away the entire field of conventional purchasing techniques, seemingly overnight. Took a twelve months' leave-of-absence (with pay, thanks to the generosity of my Board of Directors) to attend both British and American technical schools for the purpose of learning about computers.

Learn I did, quickly enough to recognize that almost any computer hardware would be adequate but there was nowhere in existence even the basis of the software we'd need. The nature of purchasing in a free market economy must contain a large element of prediction if it's going to succeed. For example, an order entered on the London Metals Exchange for 5000 ounces of platinum at $821 per ounce is justified if the price is the lowest available at the time of sale. However, if 24 hours later identical product could be bought for $790.50 per ounce on the West Coast Metals Market in America, temporarily justified or not, the London placement was a bad buy. It was simply and over-spending of $152,500 on a transaction.

The Internal Audit Committee of the Board of Directors, although they'd call the loss 62,000 pounds, wouldn't be at all happy with the London transaction. A couple of these and the old Christmas bonus is likely to be in tatters. In order to prevent this, we needed to create a software system with enough sophistication to handle justification of a group of competing trends and make a market estimate on an hourly basis based on collation of the differing data. Only in this way could we detect small variations which would allow us to predict price direction at the beginning of a short term cycle.

Took nearly three years to do and another year to check in full operation; at that time, everybody from the Chairman of the Board to the newest computer programmer agreed on one thing. Within stated limitations our program produced the most reliable short term predictions of random events on this planet. The problems of purchasing were clearing up...maybe I could spend less time on airplanes.

The question Maeve asked me one evening I recognized as sheer serendipity. "Is there a way we can tell which of our horses should be run on a certain day?" The last thing one wants to do is run horses that finish in a dead heat with other horses one owns. We coded conditions that would affect a race and punched in all previous data for each horse. We then coded the predicted conditions, weather, state of turf, etc. and pushed the proper buttons. The system worked well enough that "no prediction" occurred less than 3% of the time.

Over a year's running, using our own stable and several stables owned by friends, we amassed enough data that we had to assign a category we called "theoretical error" because we weren't sure exactly what it was. In a number of cases, the prediction made was not in line with performance; this was especially true when the computer was forced to reject one of two strong candidates. It didn't take long before we began to think about the people who handled the horses; racing is, at least, a team effort.

Correspondence with jockey clubs, turf associations, newspapers and other sources picked up literally thousands of histories of performance of riders still active as well as classic riders retired. While we were dividing data to decide how best to punch it into the computer, Maeve suggested that instead .of individual birthdates we use the conventional zodiac time periods. She had a slight interest in astrology. I had none, but using birth signs would reduce the problem of entry dates from 365 to 12. A primary rule for any computer program: Simplify.

With nothing in mind but producing the simplest possible program, we set up a key for a lock we hadn't planned to open. In a very few weeks, it was apparent that the computer predictions based on past data corresponded very closely with what could have been predicted from astrological charts. In a few double blind tests, we used astrological data exclusively and found again a close co-relation to computer predictive curves.

This answered Maeve's query to her satisfaction by reducing to almost zero the number of future races in which two of her horses would compete. But it raised a further question for me. With the software systems available, all I needed was raw data to be able to offer a reliable prediction on the relationship between the date and time and the chance of backing a winner for an individual bettor.

Using word of mouth, newspaper advertising and direct mail solicitation we managed in six months to accumulate several thousand response cards. (Enough, friends who are pollsters tell me, to constitute more than six times the number required to make the sample valid for the entire British Isles.) The cards were coded and run into the system and it became apparent that luck, whatever else it is, is a cyclic thing with individuals and that the cycle is short and very irregular. (There is some evidence that a long-term cycle also exists. Maybe a few more research years will dig it out.) Another thing that became apparent is that luck is generic. We could find no case where a person was a consistent winner with horses and loser at other games in the same time period.

To check this we had agents play fan-tan in Soho, dice and roulette in Monte Carlo, poker in Gardena and keno in Reno. The data confirmed what we originally predicted - that there are cycles in luck that somehow are connected with the astrological cycle and that these cycles could be predicted broken into very short and precise time intervals. And that this data, as reproduced in YOUR LUCKY STARS, if properly used, would greatly increase a bettor's possibility of winning in games of chance.

Costa Del Sol
June, 1983

YOUR LUCKY STARS
INTRODUCTION
STARFALL, GAMING AND GOLD

Anybody who's used one recognizes the graphite tennis racket as an excellent tool. Dimensionally stable, recovery time short enough to put all your power behind a shot, light enough for the longest match on the hottest day. But it makes a lousy hammer. All good tools are this way; a tool that attempts to do everything doesn't do anything very well. An excellent tool is intended to do one thing as well as it can be done.

YOUR LUCKY STARS is an excellent tool. It is designed to point out your relative probability at winning in any game of chance in which you might engage. It provides this information accurately for three time periods covering 24 hours of each day of the year. One thousand and ninety five times during the year your charts alert you to the ebb and flow of your luck. This is everything YOUR LUCKY STARS does. If you want information on your sex life, real estate transactions or your possibilities of traveling to foreign lands YOUR LUCKY STARS won't help a damn bit. There are books available which contend they can

1

help you with all the problem areas of your life. Maybe they can. YOUR LUCKY STARS doesn't try; we simply don't believe that beating in a nail with a graphite racket makes it a hammer.

We want to do one thing right. We believe that we have. But putting precise information in place for use is only half the job. You, the reader, must supply the other half. YLS has to be used and correctly used for you to get the maximum benefit from it. There will be a few people who will buy a copy of the book, go through it until they find an extremely lucky period. They'll place a bet, hit, which will a lot more than pay for the book, brag for a week or two and then forget it. These people are below average gamblers.

Average isn't a lot better. Nick the Turk used to say, "Average gambler arrives in Vegas in a $12,000 Oldsmobile, leaves in a $500,000 Greyhound bus." This is a shorthand way of saying the average gambler doesn't know enough about the game he's playing to know when not to play. Anyone who knows even a little about gaming can get information on whether he ought to play with a short run of cards or dice. (Costs a lot less to get it from YLS). If you don't know the game you plan to play, take time to learn it. The casino already knows the game. Christians don't seem to have much to do with gambling one way or another, but one rendering of the Crucifixion scene shows two Roman soldiers throwing dice for Christ's robe. Wasn't a new game then.

This is simply saying that no matter what your luck sign shows, you can never get lucky enough over a long period to overcome bad bets. If you draw to inside straights, bet the "Big 6 & Big 8", split face cards, bet the longest shots you can find in parlays, you ain't gonna be a winner. YOUR LUCKY STARS is written in conservative figures because to do otherwise would be irresponsible. YLS assumes a "worst case" philosophy; this means simply that the state of your luck might be a little better than shown for small time interval in some periods covered. More importantly it means your luck will never be less good than the luck sign shown, even momentarily, in the period covered. In order to be sure of this, the calculations in this book took hundreds of extra hours after theory said its accuracy was excellent. This was done to be sure that the user of YLS has at his command as wide an advantage as we can give him. It's up to the user to translate that advantage into action. Very few people, knowing little about golf, would challenge Jack Nicklaus at $500 a hole; no such intelligence is shown at the craps table.

In any gaming, the challenger (the person who makes the bet) is playing against professionals with experience of centuries and with house rules designed to bolster the natural advantage to the casino. Might be well here to note that if you're playing in an unfamiliar casino, it's a good idea to check the rules the house uses in your game. Ain't going to be a big change but it might be enough to cost you a bet or two. Just

3

not safe to assume Black Jack is played by identical rules in Indian Wells, Nevada, and in Atlantic City, N.J. When you get the rules, think about them for a minute. If you don't like 'em, don't play. The house isn't going to listen to any argument about the way its rules are established. In most places, the one you don't like isn't the only game in town.

Another thing to keep in mind when gaming. Ain't no rush. You don't have to bet every come-out on dice; if somebody else opened and you couldn't, might be an excellent place to start not playing pocker. The wheel will roll even if your bet isn't down. A lot of so-called "bettors mistakes" aren't mistakes at all. The bettor lets himself get caught up in the foolishness of becoming an automaton and feeding chips into a game without thinking about each bet carefully. Somewhere down the line he discovers to his horrer he's managed to get on both the back and front lines and his run of luck reduces to zero. Not to take the time you need to make a proper decision on your bet is foolish.

If you have a tendency to crowd your play, consider YLS. It is essentially about time; the amassing of the data of century upon century of astrological knowledge. Then the slow and tedious process of extracting knowlege by comparing small individual pieces of information (bytes) with the generic rules established by centuries of obser- vation. It is only in very recent times that this could be done. An attempt to produce this knowledge with the equipment in use even three decades ago would have been impossible. What this says is that both the accreting and evaluating of raw information began on an incredibly massive scale, but extreme care was taken to achieve accuracy. As the scale reduced, accuracy did not. YSL is as accurate as it is possible to make it. The information available to you is a first in the field of gaming. As the ultimate inheritor of this code of accuracy, do your best to use the information carefully to influence the way you go about your gaming. YSL can make a large difference if you're knowledgeable and careful enough to let it.

While we're talking about time, we ought to cover a very simple rule implicit in YLS. It is this: the time segment shown in the chart is the time at which the gaming itself takes place. For instance, if a person in Los Angeles places a bet on a Mets home game, he should, because of the three hour time difference, consider what his chart says about his luck sign in the time slot in which the game is actually played. Although he hasn't left the Pacific time zone, the effect is the same as if he were personally at the event. With major sports events taking place almost every weekend in places as divergent as Wimbledon and the Hong Kong Sports Arena, it's a good habit to check time differentials and obtain a chart reading on what the actual playing time of the event is in your location.

Let's recap briefly the other things you have to know and remember to allow YLS to improve your gaming results:

I

YLS is useable only for gaming. It is based on math that is associated with chance. Hence, won't be of any help in controlled situations: picking a mate, making an investment, etc.

II

YLS is not a substitute for the knowledge of your game that you must have. A man, on the luckiest day of his life, might step out of the 20th floor window and land uninjured. But reasonable men don't depend on doing it.

III

If you don't know the house rules, find them out before you make a wager. You don't like them, don't pay.

IV

Don't get into a rush. If you make bets without careful calculation, you could reduce your effort by throwing the same amount of money out a bus window.

V

Consider the influence of the local time at the gaming site before deciding on a wager of your money. Whether you are present at the contest or not, your money is bet on any event possible taking place in a time period different from the one you're in.

There are a few other things we'd like to mention. One, because of the popularity of the bet, is the parlay. As you may be aware, this is the first year in which we have been able to reduce the multiplex math of astrology to useable proportions. We had hoped to be able to provide some information on parlays but the analysis is massive enough that we cannot delay publication of this book to include it. The 1985 edition will have the information required for successful parlays. The general information we can offer on the basis of first run numbers is:

1) Unless parlays transcend a twenty-four hour period, they seem to be no different than other bets.

2) No bet (parlay or not) should be placed in a below average luck period.

3) An unlucky sign anywhere along the line at event time should negate a parlay.

4) If events take place in differing time zones, be sure of your luck sign before wagering.

5) Betting a unit you wouldn't otherwise because you have a strong luck sign for each day of the parlay is unwise. Two favorites and a long shot produce a lot of excitement but only very rarely money.

Secondly, be sure your bet is a chance bet before you use YLS to determine a luck sign. A bet on a presidential candidate, although it is a yes or no proposition bet, isn't one controlled by chance. Almost every facet of the political process is susceptible to some kind of control; and if the ultimate determination of an event is within the control of man, YLS will not help with any decision.

Third and last, two of man's oldest superstitions enter into gambling. The first just doesn't exist; it's called fairness. Nobody has ever said any element of life is fair. Because A gets something doesn't mean B can expect it also. One element that proceeds from the concept of "fairness" bugs inexperienced gamblers and sometimes haunts experienced ones. This element is called "average." It's easy to believe that because a flipped coin has produced five heads in a row, the next flip favors a showing of tails. Unfortunately, it isn't so.

A coin has no memory of what side last showed - it has two sides and on flip #1 and flip #200 the odds on the fall being heads or tails are the same: even money. There comes a day when you feel you ought to win; YLS doesn't say it's your day but you've got the feeling. So you go from game to game and nothing works. You don't lose big, you just lose. This is the way the concept of "average" sneaks in against a player who's too experienced to let it bug him in his bets at the table.

There's no way to say you can't ever win on a day in which your luck sign is below average. If you make a bet with a guy whose luck is even worse than yours on a given day, you've probably got a winner. What the hell, you can't both lose. If you pick a 100-1 shot, or draw three cards to a flush because you have a far above average luck sign, you probably have a loser. In order to organize YLS into something useful for people who enjoy gaming, it had to have a starting point. Oddly enough, the starting point for average luck was based on the results of what the average guy would achieve. For determing the average, we assumed four things:

1) The bettor had no knowledge to which all other bettors weren't privy.

2) The bettor could not wager enough money to change odds on the event.

3) The bettor knew enough about his game to avoid making a "bonehead" bet.

4) The bettor placed his wager in the proper time frame.

YOUR LUCKY STARS was published for you. If you use it properly, you will be a winner.

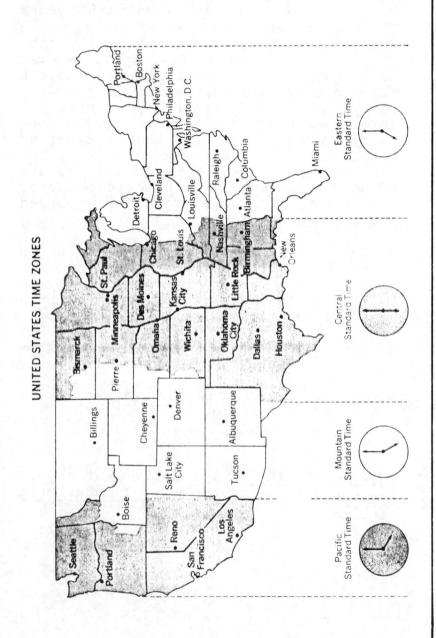

UNITED STATES TIME ZONES

Eastern Standard Time

Central Standard Time

Mountain Standard Time

Pacific Standard Time

10

YOUR LUCKY STARS

1984

Division of Day Into Portions	SUN 1	MON 2	TUE 3	WED 4	THU 5	FRI 6	SAT 7
12:00M-12:00N	1 BB	1 A	1 A	1AA	1 A	1 A	1 B
12:00N-6:00PM	2 A	2 A	2AA	2 A	2 BB	2 A	2 A
6:00PM-12:00M	3 A	3 A	3 W	3 A	3 A	3 A	3 AA

LEO jul 23 - aug 22	SUN 1	MON 2	TUE 3	WED 4	THU 5	FRI 6	SAT 7
	1 A	1 A	1 A	1 A	1 BB	1 BB	1 A
	2 A	2 A	2 A	2 A	2 BB	2 A	2 A
	3 A	3 A	3 A	3 BB	3 BB	3 A	3 A

VIRGO aug 23 - sep 22	SUN 1	MON 2	TUE 3	WED 4	THU 5	FRI 6	SAT 7
	1BB	1 BB	1 A	1AA	1 A	1 A	1 A
	2BB	2 A	2 A	2AA	2 A	2AA	2 A
	3BB	3 A	3 A	3 A	3 A	3 AA	3 A

LIBRA sep 23 - oct 22	SUN 1	MON 2	TUE 3	WED 4	THU 5	FRI 6	SAT 7
	1 AA	1 AA	1 A	1 A	1 AA	1 A	1 A
	2 AA	2 AA	2 A	2 A	2 AA	2 A	2 A
	3 AA	3 A	3 A	3 A	3 W	3 A	3 A

SCORPIO oct 23 - nov 22	SUN 1	MON 2	TUE 3
	1 A	1 A	1BB
	2 A	2 B	2BB
	3 A	3 B	3BB

SAGITTARIUS nov 23 - dec 21	SUN 1	MON 2	TUE 3
	1 A	1 A	1 A
	2 A	2 A	2 A
	3 A	3 A	3 A

Letter Values
(luck signs)
A-Average
AA-Above average
W-Far above average
B-Below average
BB-Far below average
X-Very far below average

11

your Lucky stars
January 1-7
1984

CAPRICORN δec 22 - jan 19	SUN 1	MON 2	TUE 3	WED 4	THU 5	FRI 6	SAT 7
	1 A	1 A	1 AA	1A	1A	1 B	1 A
	2 A	2 A	2 AA	2A	2W	2 B	2 A
	3 A	3A	3 A	3A	3B	3 B	3A

AQUARIUS jan 20 - feb 19	SUN 1	MON 2	TUE 3	WED 4	THU 5	FRI 6	SAT 7
	1 B	1 A	1 A	1 B	1AA	1 A	1 A
	2 B	2 A	2 B	2A	2A	2A	2A
	3 A	3A	3 B	3A	3A	3 A	3 B

PISCES feb 20 - mar 20	SUN 1	MON 2	TUE 3	WED 4	THU 5	FRI 6	SAT 7
	1 B	1 B	1 B	1 A	1 A	1 B	1 B
	2 B	2 B	2A	2 A	2A	2 B	2B
	3 B	3 B	3A	3 A	3A	3 B	3A

ARIES mar 21 - apr 19	SUN 1	MON 2	TUE 3	WED 4	THU 5	FRI 6	SAT 7
	1BB	1BB	1B	1 A	1 A	1 A	1 B
	2BB	2 BB	2B	2 A	2 A	2A	2 B
	3BB	3X	3B	3 A	3 A	3 B	3A

TAURUS apr 20 - may 20	SUN 1	MON 2	TUE 3	WED 4	THU 5	FRI 6	SAT 7
	1A	1AA	1 A	1 A	1 A	1 A	1 A
	2A	2AA	2 A	2 A	2 A	2 A	2A
	3AA	3 A	3 A	3 A	3 A	3 A	3A

GEMINI may 21 - jun 20	SUN 1	MON 2	TUE 3	WED 4	THU 5	FRI 6	SAT 7
	1 A	1 A	1 AA	1 A	1 A	1 B	1 B
	2 A	2A	2 AA	2 A	2A	2 B	2A
	3 A	3A	3 A	3 A	3A	3 B	3 A

YOUR LUCKY STARS
January 1-7
1984

CANCER Jun 21 - Jul 22	SUN 1	MON 2	TUE 3	WED 4	THU 5	FRI 6	SAT 7
	1 BB	1 A	1A	1AA	1 A	1 A	1 B
	2 A	2 A	2AA	2 A	2 BB	2 A	2 A
	3 A	3 A	3W	3 A	3 A	3 A	3 AA

LEO Jul 23 - Aug 22	SUN 1	MON 2	TUE 3	WED 4	THU 5	FRI 6	SAT 7
	1 A	1 A	1 A	1 A	1 BB	1 BB	1 A
	2 A	2 A	2 A	2 A	2 BB	2 A	2 A
	3 A	3 A	3 A	3 BB	3 BB	3 A	3 A

VIRGO Aug 23 - Sep 22	SUN 1	MON 2	TUE 3	WED 4	THU 5	FRI 6	SAT 7
	1 BB	1 BB	1A	1AA	1 A	1 A	1 A
	2 BB	2 A	2 A	2AA	2 A	2 AA	2 A
	3 BB	3 A	3 A	3A	3 A	3 AA	3 A

LIBRA Sep 23 - Oct 22	SUN 1	MON 2	TUE 3	WED 4	THU 5	FRI 6	SAT 7
	1 AA	1 AA	1 A	1 A	1 AA	1 A	1 A
	2 AA	2 AA	2 A	2 A	2 AA	2 A	2 A
	3 AA	3 A	3 A	3 A	3W	3 A	3 A

SCORPIO Oct 23 - Nov 22	SUN 1	MON 2	TUE 3	WED 4	THU 5	FRI 6	SAT 7
	1 A	1 A	1 BB	1X	1 BB	1 BB	1 A
	2 A	2 B	2 BB	2 BB	2 BB	2 A	2 A
	3 A	3 B	3 BB	3 BB	3 BB	3 A	3 A

SAGITTARIUS Nov 23 - Dec 21	SUN 1	MON 2	TUE 3	WED 4	THU 5	FRI 6	SAT 7
	1 A	1 A	1 A	1 BB	1 BB	1 AA	1 A
	2 A	2 A	2 A	2 BB	2 A	2 AA	2 A
	3 A	3 A	3 A	3 BB	3 A	3 A	3 A

13

your lucky stars
January 8-14
1984

CAPRICORN dec 22 - jan 19	SUN 8	MON 9	TUE 10	WED 11	THU 12	FRI 13	SAT 14
	1 A	1 A	1 A	1 B	1B	1B	1 A
	2 AA	2 A	2 B	2B	2B	2 A	2 A
	3 A	3 A	3 B	3B	3B	3A	3A

aquarius jan 20 - feb 19	SUN 8	MON 9	TUE 10	WED 11	THU 12	FRI 13	SAT 14
	1 A	1 A	1 A	1 A	1 B	1 A	1 B
	2 A	2 AA	2 A	2 B	2 B	2 B	2 B
	3 A	3 AA	3 A	3 B	3 A	3 B	3BB

pisces feb 20 - mar 20	SUN 8	MON 9	TUE 10	WED 11	THU 12	FRI 13	SAT 14
	1 BB	1 BB	1 BB	1X	1AA	1AA	1 A
	2 BB	2 BB	2 BB	2 B	2AA	2A	2A
	3 BB	3 BB	3 BB	3A	3AA	3A	3A

aries mar 21 - apr 19	SUN 8	MON 9	TUE 10	WED 11	THU 12	FRI 13	SAT 14
	1 A	1 B	1 A	1AA	1 A	1 B	1B
	2 A	2 A	2 A	2 A	2AA	2 B	2 B
	3 B	3 A	3 A	3 A	3 A	3 B	3A

taurus apr 20 - may 20	SUN 8	MON 9	TUE 10	WED 11	THU 12	FRI 13	SAT 14
	1 A	1 A	1 A	1 B	1AA	1AA	1B
	2 A	2 A	2 B	2A	2 A	2 A	2A
	3 A	3 A	3 B	3A	3W	3B	3A

gemini may 21 - jun 20	SUN 8	MON 9	TUE 10	WED 11	THU 12	FRI 13	SAT 14
	1 B	1 A	1 A	1 B	1 B	1AA	1 A
	2 B	2 A	2 A	2 B	2 A	2A	2 A
	3 A	3 A	3 A	3 B	3AA	3A	3 A

youR lucky staRs
January 8-14
1984

CANCER Jun 21 - Jul 22	SUN 8	MON 9	TUE 10	WED 11	THU 12	FRI 13	SAT 14
	1BB	1B	1A	1A	1B	1B	1A
	2BB	2B	2A	2A	2B	2B	2A
	3BB	3A	3A	3B	3B	3A	3B

LEO Jul 23 - aug 22	SUN 8	MON 9	TUE 10	WED 11	THU 12	FRI 13	SAT 14
	1A	1A	1A	1A	1B	1B	1A
	2A	2A	2A	2A	2B	2B	2A
	3A	3A	3A	3B	3B	3B	3AA

VIRGO aug 23 - sep 22	SUN 8	MON 9	TUE 10	WED 11	THU 12	FRI 13	SAT 14
	1B	1B	1B	1BB	1A	1B	1B
	2B	2B	2BB	2B	2A	2BB	2B
	3B	3B	3BB	3B	3A	3BB	3B

LIBRA sep 23 - oct 22	SUN 8	MON 9	TUE 10	WED 11	THU 12	FRI 13	SAT 14
	1A	1A	1A	1B	1A	1AA	1A
	2A	2A	2B	2A	2A	2A	2A
	3A	3A	3B	3A	3A	3A	3A

SCORPIO oct 23 - nov 22	SUN 8	MON 9	TUE 10	WED 11	THU 12	FRI 13	SAT 14
	1AA	1A	1A	1B	1A	1A	1A
	2AA	2A	2A	2B	2A	2A	2B
	3A	3A	3A	3A	3A	3A	3B

SAGITTARIUS nov 23 - dec 21	SUN 8	MON 9	TUE 10	WED 11	THU 12	FRI 13	SAT 14
	1B	1A	1A	1AA	1A	1A	1B
	2B	2A	2A	2AA	2A	2B	2A
	3A	3A	3A	3A	3A	3B	3A

your lucky stars
January 15-21
1984

CAPRICORN dec 22 - jan 19	SUN 15	MON 16	TUE 17	WED 18	THU 19	FRI 20	SAT 21
	1B	1A	1A	1A	1A	1B	1B
	2A	2A	2AA	2A	2B	2B	2A
	3A	3A	3AA	3A	3B	3B	3A

AQUARIUS jan 20 - feb 19	SUN 15	MON 16	TUE 17	WED 18	THU 19	FRI 20	SAT 21
	1B	1BB	1B	1A	1B	1B	1B
	2BB	2BB	2B	2B	2BB	2B	2B
	3BB	3BB	3A	3B	3X	3B	3A

PISCES feb 20 - mar 20	SUN 15	MON 16	TUE 17	WED 18	THU 19	FRI 20	SAT 21
	1A	1AA	1AA	1A	1B	1A	1AA
	2A	2AA	2A	2B	2B	2A	2A
	3A	3AA	3A	3B	3A	3A	3A

ARIES mar 21 - apr 19	SUN 15	MON 16	TUE 17	WED 18	THU 19	FRI 20	SAT 21
	1B	1A	1A	1B	1A	1AA	1A
	2B	2A	2A	2B	2A	2A	2A
	3A	3A	3A	3A	3A	3A	3A

TAURUS apr 20 - may 20	SUN 15	MON 16	TUE 17	WED 18	THU 19	FRI 20	SAT 21
	1A	1B	1BB	1BB	1B	1A	1A
	2A	2B	2BB	2B	2A	2A	2A
	3B	3B	3BB	3B	3A	3A	3B

GEMINI may 21 - jun 20	SUN 15	MON 16	TUE 17	WED 18	THU 19	FRI 20	SAT 21
	1BB	1A	1A	1AA	1A	1B	1A
	2A	2A	2A	2AA	2A	2B	2A
	3A	3A	3A	3A	3B	3B	3B

your lucky stars

January 15-21

1984

	SUN 15	MON 16	TUE 17	WED 18	THU 19	FRI 20	SAT 21
CANCER Jun 21 - Jul 22	1 A 2 A 3 A	1 A 2 A 3 A	1 A 2 B 3 B	1 BB 2 BB 3 B	1 A 2 A 3 A	1 A 2 A 3 A	1 A 2 B 3 B
LEO Jul 23 - Aug 22	1 B 2 B 3 B	1 B 2 B 3 B	1 A 2 A 3 A	1 A 2 A 3 A	1 A 2 A 3 A	1 A 2 A 3 A	1 A 2 A 3 A
VIRGO Aug 23 - Sep 22	1 A 2 A 3 A	1 A 2 A 3 B	1 BB 2 BB 3 BB	1 BB 2 B 3 B	1 B 2 B 3 B	1 A 2 A 3 A	1 A 2 A 3 B
LIBRA Sep 23 - Oct 22	1 B 2 A 3 A	1 A 2 A 3 A	1 A 2 A 3 B	1 B 2 B 3 B	1 BB 2 BB 3 BB	1 BB 2 BB 3 BB	1 BB 2 BB 3 BB
SCORPIO Oct 23 - Nov 22	1 BB 2 BB 3 BB	1 BB 2 BB 3 B	1 B 2 B 3 B	1 B 2 A 3 A	1 A 2 A 3 A	1 BB 2 BB 3 B	1 X 2 X 3 B
SAGITTARIUS Nov 23 - Dec 21	1 B 2 A 3 A	1 A 2 A 3 A	1 B 2 B 3 B	1 B 2 B 3 B	1 A 2 A 3 A	1 A 2 AA 3 B	1 B 2 B 3 A

your lucky stars
January 22-28
1984

CAPRICORN δεc 22 - jan 19	SUN 22	MON 23	TUE 24	WED 25	THU 26	FRI 27	SAT 28
	1 A	1 B	1 A	1 A	1 B	1 B	1 BB
	2 B	2 B	2 A	2 A	2 B	2 B	2 BB
	3 B	3 A	3 A	3 B	3 B	3 BB	3 BB

AQUARIUS jan 20 - feb 19	SUN 22	MON 23	TUE 24	WED 25	THU 26	FRI 27	SAT 28
	1A	1 A	1 A	1 B	1 A	1 A	1B
	2A	2 A	2 B	2 A	2 AA	2 A	2B
	3A	3 A	3 B	3 A	3 A	3 A	3B

PISCES feb 20 - mar 20	SUN 22	MON 23	TUE 24	WED 25	THU 26	FRI 27	SAT 28
	1 B	1 B	1 BB	1 B	1 A	1 A	1 B
	2 A	2 B	2 BB	2 B	2 A	2 A	2B
	3 A	3 B	3 B	3 A	3 A	3 B	3B

ARIES mar 21 - apr 19	SUN 22	MON 23	TUE 24	WED 25	THU 26	FRI 27	SAT 28
	1 B	1 A	1A	1 A	1 B	1 B	1 B
	2 B	2 A	2AA	2 BB	2 B	2 B	2 B
	3 A	3 A	3A	3 B	3 B	3 B	3 B

TAURUS apr 20 - may 20	SUN 22	MON 23	TUE 24	WED 25	THU 26	FRI 27	SAT 28
	1 B	1 A	1AA	1 AA	1 A	1 B	1 B
	2 A	2 A	2AA	2 A	2 A	2 B	2 B
	3 A	3 A	3AA	3 A	3 B	3 B	3 BB

GEMINI may 21 - jun 20	SUN 22	MON 23	TUE 24	WED 25	THU 26	FRI 27	SAT 28
	1 B	1 B	1 B	1 B	1 B	1 A	1 A
	2 B	2 B	2 B	2 B	2 B	2 A	2 A
	3 B	3 B	3 B	3 B	3 A	3 A	3 A

18

YOUR LUCKY STARS
January 22-28
1984

CANCER
Jun 21 - Jul 22

	SUN 22	MON 23	TUE 24	WED 25	THU 26	FRI 27	SAT 28
1	1 A	1 A	1 B	1 BB	1 A	1 A	1 A
2	2 AA	2 A	2 B	2 A	2 A	2 A	2 A
3	3 A	3 A	3 B	3 A	3 A	3 A	3 B

LEO
Jul 23 - Aug 22

	SUN 22	MON 23	TUE 24	WED 25	THU 26	FRI 27	SAT 28
1	1 B	1 B	1 A	1 A	1 A	1 W	1 B
2	2 B	2 B	2 A	2 A	2 A	2 A	2 B
3	3 B	3 A	3 A	3 A	3 A	3 B	3 B

VIRGO
Aug 23 - Sep 22

	SUN 22	MON 23	TUE 24	WED 25	THU 26	FRI 27	SAT 28
1	1 B	1 A	1 AA	1 AA	1 AA	1 A	1 A
2	2 A	2 A	2 A	2 A	2 A	2 B	2 A
3	3 A	3 A	3 A	3 A	3 A	3 B	3 A

LIBRA
Sep 23 - Oct 22

	SUN 22	MON 23	TUE 24	WED 25	THU 26	FRI 27	SAT 28
1	1 BB	1 B	1 B	1 B	1 A	1 A	1 B
2	2 BB	2 B	2 B	2 B	2 A	2 A	2 B
3	3 BB	3 B	3 B	3 B	3 A	3 B	3 A

SCORPIO
Oct 23 - Nov 22

	SUN 22	MON 23	TUE 24	WED 25	THU 26	FRI 27	SAT 28
1	1 A	1 A	1 B	1 BB	1 B	1 A	1 A
2	2 A	2 A	2 B	2 BB	2 B	2 A	2 A
3	3 A	3 A	3 B	3 B	3 A	3 A	3 AA

SAGITTARIUS
Nov 23 - Dec 21

	SUN 22	MON 23	TUE 24	WED 25	THU 26	FRI 27	SAT 28
1	1 B	1 A	1 A	1 B	1 B	1 B	1 B
2	2 B	2 AA	2 B	2 B	2 B	2 B	2 B
3	3 A	3 AA	3 B	3 B	3 B	3 B	3 B

your lucky stars

January 29-February 4

1984

CAPRICORN
δεc 22 - jan 19

	SUN 29	MON 30	TUE 31	WED 1	THU 2	FRI 3	SAT 4
1	BB	B	B	B	A	A	B
2	B	B	BB	B	A	A	B
3	B	B	BB	A	A	B	B

AQUARIUS
jan 20 - feb 19

	SUN 29	MON 30	TUE 31	WED 1	THU 2	FRI 3	SAT 4
1	A	A	AA	A	A	A	A
2	A	A	AA	A	A	A	A
3	A	A	A	A	A	A	A

PISCES
feb 20 - mar 20

	SUN 29	MON 30	TUE 31	WED 1	THU 2	FRI 3	SAT 4
1	A	B	BB	A	A	A	A
2	A	B	B	A	A	A	A
3	B	B	A	A	A	A	A

ARIES
mar 21 - apr 19

	SUN 29	MON 30	TUE 31	WED 1	THU 2	FRI 3	SAT 4
1	B	A	B	A	A	A	A
2	A	B	B	A	A	AA	A
3	A	B	B	A	A	AA	A

TAURUS
apr 20 - may 20

	SUN 29	MON 30	TUE 31	WED 1	THU 2	FRI 3	SAT 4
1	AA	AA	A	A	B	B	B
2	AA	A	A	A	B	B	A
3	AA	A	A	B	B	B	A

GEMINI
may 21 - jun 20

	SUN 29	MON 30	TUE 31	WED 1	THU 2	FRI 3	SAT 4
1	BB	A	A	A	A	A	A
2	BB	A	A	A	A	A	A
3	A	A	A	A	A	A	A

20

YOUR LUCKY STARS

January 29-February 4

1984

CANCER
jun 21 - jul 22

	SUN 29	MON 30	TUE 31	WED 1	THU 2	FRI 3	SAT 4
	1 A	1 B	1A	1 A	1 AA	1 AA	1 A
	2 A	2 B	2A	2 A	2 AA	2 A	2 A
	3 B	3 A	3A	3 A	3 AA	3 A	3A

LEO
jul 23 - aug 22

	SUN 29	MON 30	TUE 31	WED 1	THU 2	FRI 3	SAT 4
	1 B	1 B	1BB	1 B	1 A	1 A	1 A
	2 B	2 B	2BB	2 A	2 A	2 A	2 A
	3 B	3 BB	3B	3 A	3 A	3 A	3 A

VIRGO
aug 23 - sep 22

	SUN 29	MON 30	TUE 31	WED 1	THU 2	FRI 3	SAT 4
	1AA	1 A	1 A	1 A	1 A	1 AA	1AA
	2AA	2 A	2A	2 A	2 A	2 AA	2A
	3A	3 A	3A	3 A	3 AA	3 AA	3A

LIBRA
sep 23 - oct 22

	SUN 29	MON 30	TUE 31	WED 1	THU 2	FRI 3	SAT 4
	1 A	1 B	1A	1 A	1 A	1 B	1 BB
	2 B	2B	2A	2 A	2 A	2 B	2 BB
	3 B	3 B	3A	3 A	3 A	3 BB	3 B

SCORPIO
oct 23 - nov 22

	SUN 29	MON 30	TUE 31	WED 1	THU 2	FRI 3	SAT 4
	1 A	1 A	1 A	1 W	1 A	1 A	1 A
	2 A	2 A	2 AA	2 W	2 A	2A	2 A
	3A	3A	3 AA	3 AA	3 A	3 A	3A

SAGITTARIUS
nov 23 - dec 21

	SUN 29	MON 30	TUE 31	WED 1	THU 2	FRI 3	SAT 4
	1 B	1A	1 A	1 A	1 B	1 B	1A
	2B	2A	2 A	2 B	2 B	2 A	2B
	3B	3A	3 A	3 B	3 BB	3A	3 B

your Lucky stars

February 5-11

1984

CAPRICORN δec 22 - jan 19	SUN 5	MON 6	TUE 7	WED 8	THU 9	FRI 10	SAT 11
	1 A	1 B	1 A	1 A	1 A	1 A	1 AA
	2 B	2 B	2 A	2 AA	2 A	2 A	2 W
	3 B	3 A	3 A	3 AA	3 A	3 A	3 A

AQUARIUS jan 20 - feb 19	SUN 5	MON 6	TUE 7	WED 8	THU 9	FRI 10	SAT 11
	1 A	1 A	1 B	1 B	1 BB	1A	1 A
	2 A	2 A	2 B	2 B	2 B	2A	2 AA
	3 A	3 B	3 B	3 B	3 A	3A	3 AA

PISCES feb 20 - mar 20	SUN 5	MON 6	TUE 7	WED 8	THU 9	FRI 10	SAT 11
	1 A	1 B	1 B	1 A	1 A	1 BB	1 BB
	2 B	2 B	2 A	2 B	2 A	2 BB	2 BB
	3 B	3 B	3 A	3 B	3 B	3 BB	3 B

ARIES mar 21 - apr 19	SUN 5	MON 6	TUE 7	WED 8	THU 9	FRI 10	SAT 11
	1 B	1 A	1 A	1 B	1 B	1 A	1 A
	2 B	2 A	2 A	2 B	2 BB	2 A	2 AA
	3 A	3 A	3 B	3 A	3 B	3 A	3 A

TAURUS apr 20 - may 20	SUN 5	MON 6	TUE 7	WED 8	THU 9	FRI 10	SAT 11
	1 AA	1 A	1 A	1 A	1AA	1 B	1 B
	2 AA	2 A	2 B	2 A	2A	2 B	2 A
	3 AA	3 A	3 B	3 AA	3 A	3 B	3 A

GEMINI may 21 - jun 20	SUN 5	MON 6	TUE 7	WED 8	THU 9	FRI 10	SAT 11
	1A	1 A	1 A	1 BB	1 A	1 B	1 A
	2A	2 AA	2 A	2 B	2 A	2 B	2 A
	3A	3 A	3 B	3 B	3 B	3 A	3 A

your lucky stars
February 5-11
1984

CANCER Jun 21 - Jul 22	SUN 5	MON 6	TUE 7	WED 8	THU 9	FRI 10	SAT 11
	1 B	1 A	1 A	1 A	1 AA	1 A	1 B
	2 B	2 A	2 AA	2 A	2 A	2 B	2 B
	3 A	3 A	3 A	3 AA	3 A	3 B	3 B

LEO Jul 23 - Aug 22	SUN 5	MON 6	TUE 7	WED 8	THU 9	FRI 10	SAT 11
	1 A	1 A	1 A	1 A	1 BB	1A	1 B
	2 B	2 A	2 A	2 B	2BB	2A	2 B
	3 A	3 A	3 A	3 B	3A	3B	3 A

VIRGO Aug 23 - Sep 22	SUN 5	MON 6	TUE 7	WED 8	THU 9	FRI 10	SAT 11
	1 B	1 B	1 B	1 BB	1 A	1B	1 A
	2 B	2 B	2 B	2 BB	2 A	2B	2 A
	3 B	3 B	3BB	3 B	3 B	3A	3 AA

LIBRA Sep 23 - Oct 22	SUN 5	MON 6	TUE 7	WED 8	THU 9	FRI 10	SAT 11
	1 A	1 B	1 A	1 A	1BB	1 B	1 BB
	2 A	2 B	2 A	2 B	2BB	2 X	2 BB
	3 B	3 A	3 A	3 B	3BB	3 X	3 B

SCORPIO Oct 23 - Nov 22	SUN 5	MON 6	TUE 7	WED 8	THU 9	FRI 10	SAT 11
	1 A	1 B	1 A	1 AA	1 B	1A	1 B
	2 B	2 A	2 A	2 A	2 B	2B	2 B
	3 B	3 A	3A	3 B	3A	3B	3 B

SAGITTARIUS Nov 23 - Dec 21	SUN 5	MON 6	TUE 7	WED 8	THU 9	FRI 10	SAT 11
	1 A	1 A	1 A	1 A	1 B	1 A	1 B
	2 A	2 A	2 AA	2 A	2 B	2 A	2 B
	3 A	3 A	3 AA	3 B	3 B	3 B	3 B

your lucky stars
February 12-18
1984

CAPRICORN Dec 22 - Jan 19	SUN 12	MON 13	TUE 14	WED 15	THU 16	FRI 17	SAT 18
	1 BB	1 A	1 A	1 A	1 B	1 B	1 B
	2 B	2 A	2 A	2 B	2 A	2 BB	2 A
	3 A	3 A	3 A	3 B	3 A	3 B	3 A

AQUARIUS Jan 20 - Feb 19	SUN 12	MON 13	TUE 14	WED 15	THU 16	FRI 17	SAT 18
	1A	1A	1A	1 AA	1 A	1 B	1AA
	2A	2A	2A	2AA	2 B	2 A	2W
	3A	3A	3A	3A	3 B	3 B	3A

PISCES Feb 20 - Mar 20	SUN 12	MON 13	TUE 14	WED 15	THU 16	FRI 17	SAT 18
	1 A	1B	1B	1A	1 A	1 B	1 A
	2 A	2B	2B	2A	2 A	2B	2 A
	3 A	3B	3A	3A	3 A	3A	3 AA

ARIES Mar 21 - Apr 19	SUN 12	MON 13	TUE 14	WED 15	THU 16	FRI 17	SAT 18
	1 B	1 B	1 BB	1 BB	1A	1 A	1 B
	2 B	2B	2 X	2 B	2 A	2 A	2A
	3 B	3BB	3 X	3 A	3 A	3 B	3A

TAURUS Apr 20 - May 20	SUN 12	MON 13	TUE 14	WED 15	THU 16	FRI 17	SAT 18
	1 B	1 A	1 AA	1A	1B	1 A	1 BB
	2A	2 AA	2 W	2 A	2 B	2 B	2 B
	3A	3 AA	3 A	3 B	3 A	3 B	3 A

GEMINI May 21 - Jun 20	SUN 12	MON 13	TUE 14	WED 15	THU 16	FRI 17	SAT 18
	1 A	1 B	1 B	1B	1 A	1 B	1A
	2 B	2 BB	2 B	2A	2 B	2A	2A
	3 B	3 B	3 B	3A	3 B	3A	3A

YOUR LUCKY STARS
February 12-18
1984

CANCER
Jun 21 - Jul 22

	SUN 12	MON 13	TUE 14	WED 15	THU 16	FRI 17	SAT 18
	1A	1 B	1 AA	1 B	1 B	1 A	1 B
	2A	2 A	2A	2 B	2 A	2 A	2 B
	3B	3 A	3 A	3 B	3 A	3 B	3 BB

LEO
Jul 23 - Aug 22

	SUN 12	MON 13	TUE 14	WED 15	THU 16	FRI 17	SAT 18
	1 A	1B	1 BB	1B	1 A	1 A	1A
	2 B	2B	2BB	2 B	2 A	2 B	2 B
	3 B	3BB	3BB	3A	3 A	3 B	3 B

VIRGO
Aug 23 - Sep 22

	SUN 12	MON 13	TUE 14	WED 15	THU 16	FRI 17	SAT 18
	1 B	1 B	1 A	1 A	1 B	1B	1 A
	2 B	2 A	2 A	2 A	2 BB	2A	2AA
	3 B	3 A	3 A	3 A	3 BB	3A	3AA

LIBRA
Sep 23 - Oct 22

	SUN 12	MON 13	TUE 14	WED 15	THU 16	FRI 17	SAT 18
	1 A	1AA	1 A	1B	1AA	1 B	1 A
	2 A	2AA	2 A	2 A	2A	2 B	2 A
	3AA	3A	3 B	3 A	3 A	3A	3 B

SCORPIO
Oct 23 - Nov 22

	SUN 12	MON 13	TUE 14	WED 15	THU 16	FRI 17	SAT 18
	1A	1 B	1A	1A	1A	1 B	1A
	2 B	2 A	2A	2 B	2A	2 B	2A
	3 B	3 A	3A	3 B	3B	3 B	3A

SAGITTARIUS
Nov 23 - Dec 21

	SUN 12	MON 13	TUE 14	WED 15	THU 16	FRI 17	SAT 18
	1A	1 B	1 BB	1 B	1B	1 A	1 A
	2A	2 B	2 BB	2 B	2B	2 A	2 A
	3A	3 BB	3 B	3 B	3A	3 A	3A

YOUR LUCKY STARS
February 19-25
1984

CAPRICORN ᗧᴇᴄ 22 - ᴊᴀɴ 19	SUN 19	MON 20	TUE 21	WED 22	THU 23	FRI 24	SAT 25
	1 BB	1 B	1 A	1 B	1 A	1 B	1 B
	2 BB	2 B	2 A	2 B	2 A	2 BB	2 A
	3 BB	3 A	3 A	3 B	3 B	3 B	3 A

AQUARIUS ᴊᴀɴ 20 - ꜰᴇʙ 19	SUN 19	MON 20	TUE 21	WED 22	THU 23	FRI 24	SAT 25
	1 B	1 B	1 A	1 A	1 A	1 A	1 B
	2 A	2 B	2 A	2 B	2 A	2 B	2 A
	3 A	3 A	3 A	3 B	3 AA	3 B	3 A

PISCES ꜰᴇʙ 20 - ᴍᴀʀ 20	SUN 19	MON 20	TUE 21	WED 22	THU 23	FRI 24	SAT 25
	1 AA	1 A	1 A	1 B	1 B	1 B	1 A
	2 A	2 A	2 AA	2 B	2 A	2 B	2 A
	3 A	3 A	3 A	3 B	3 A	3 B	3 BB

ARIES ᴍᴀʀ 21 - ᴀᴘʀ 19	SUN 19	MON 20	TUE 21	WED 22	THU 23	FRI 24	SAT 25
	1 B	1 A	1 B	1 B	1 BB	1 A	1 B
	2 B	2 A	2 B	2 BB	2 B	2 A	2 BB
	3 A	3 A	3 B	3 BB	3 B	3 B	3 B

TAURUS ᴀᴘʀ 20 - ᴍᴀʏ 20	SUN 19	MON 20	TUE 21	WED 22	THU 23	FRI 24	SAT 25
	1 A	1 A	1 A	1 A	1 B	1 B	1 B
	2 B	2 A	2 A	2 B	2 A	2 B	2 B
	3 A	3 A	3 AA	3 B	3 A	3 A	3 A

GEMINI ᴍᴀʏ 21 - ᴊᴜɴ 20	SUN 19	MON 20	TUE 21	WED 22	THU 23	FRI 24	SAT 25
	1 B	1 BB	1 A	1 B	1 A	1 BB	1 A
	2 BB	2 B	2 A	2 B	2 B	2 B	2 A
	3 X	3 A	3 A	3 A	3 B	3 A	3 A

your lucky stars
February 19-25
1984

CANCER jun 21 - jul 22	SUN 19	MON 20	TUE 21	WED 22	THU 23	FRI 24	SAT 25
	1 B	1 B	1 B	1 A	1A	1 B	1 B
	2 B	2 B	2 B	2 B	2A	2 A	2 B
	3 B	3 B	3 B	3 A	3 B	3A	3 B

LEO jul 23 - aug 22	SUN 19	MON 20	TUE 21	WED 22	THU 23	FRI 24	SAT 25
	1A	1B	1A	1 A	1 B	1A	1 B
	2A	2B	2A	2 A	2 A	2 B	2 B
	3B	3A	3A	3B	3 A	3 B	3 BB

VIRGO aug 23 - sep 22	SUN 19	MON 20	TUE 21	WED 22	THU 23	FRI 24	SAT 25
	1 A	1 B	1 B	1 A	1 A	1 B	1 A
	2 B	2 B	2 A	2 A	2 B	2 B	2 AA
	3 B	3 B	3 A	3 AA	3 B	3 A	3 W

LIBRA sep 23 - oct 22	SUN 19	MON 20	TUE 21	WED 22	THU 23	FRI 24	SAT 25
	1 BB	1 A	1 A	1 A	1 B	1 B	1 B
	2 B	2 A	2 A	2 B	2 B	2 A	2A
	3A	3 A	3 A	3 B	3 BB	3 A	3 A

SCORPIO oct 23 - nov 22	SUN 19	MON 20	TUE 21	WED 22	THU 23	FRI 24	SAT 25
	1 B	1 A	1 B	1 A	1 A	1 A	1 A
	2 B	2 B	2 BB	2 A	2 A	2 AA	2 B
	3 A	3 B	3 B	3 A	3 A	3 A	3 B

SAGITTARIUS nov 23 - dec 21	SUN 19	MON 20	TUE 21	WED 22	THU 23	FRI 24	SAT 25
	1 B	1 B	1 B	1 A	1 B	1 B	1 BB
	2 B	2 A	2 B	2 A	2 B	2 BB	2 B
	3 B	3 A	3 B	3 B	3 B	3 X	3A

27

your lucky stars
February 26-March 3
1984

CAPRICORN ᴅᴇᴄ 22 - ᴊᴀɴ 19	SUN 26	MON 27	TUE 28	WED 29	THU 1	FRI 2	SAT 3
	1 A	1 A	1 B	1 A	1 A	1 B	1B
	2 A	2 A	2A	2A	2A	2 B	2B
	3 A	3 B	3A	3A	3A	3 B	3A

AQUARIUS ᴊᴀɴ 20 - ꜰᴇʙ 19	SUN 26	MON 27	TUE 28	WED 29	THU 1	FRI 2	SAT 3
	1A	1 B	1 B	1 A	1 B	1A	1B
	2 B	2 A	2 A	2 B	2A	2A	2B
	3 B	3A	3 A	3 B	3A	3A	3B

PISCES ꜰᴇʙ 20 - ᴍᴀʀ 20	SUN 26	MON 2/	TUE 28	WED 29	THU 1	FRI 2	SAT 3
	1A	1 B	1 B	1 A	1 B	1BB	1 A
	2 A	2 B	2A	2 A	2BB	2B	2 B
	3 B	3 B	3A	3A	3BB	3A	3 B

ARIES ᴍᴀʀ 21 - ᴀᴘʀ 19	SUN 26	MON 27	TUE 28	WED 29	THU 1	FRI 2	SAT 3
	1A	1 A	1 B	1 A	1A	1 B	1 A
	2 B	2 A	2 B	2 AA	2B	2 B	2 B
	3 B	3 A	3 A	3 AA	3B	3 A	3 BB

TAURUS ᴀᴘʀ 20 - ᴍᴀʏ 20	SUN 26	MON 2/	TUE 28	WED 29	THU 1	FRI 2	SAT 3
	1A	1 A	1 A	1 B	1 A	1 X	1 B
	2A	2 AA	2 B	2A	2 B	2 BB	2B
	3A	3 AA	3 B	3A	3 BB	3 B	3A

GEMINI ᴍᴀʏ 21 - ᴊᴜɴ 20	SUN 26	MON 27	TUE 28	WED 29	THU 1	FRI 2	SAT 3
	1 AA	1 A	1 B	1A	1 A	1 B	1A
	2 AA	2 A	2 B	2A	2 B	2 B	2B
	3 AA	3 B	3A	3AA	3 B	3 B	3 B

your lucky stars

February 26-March 3

1984

CANCER Jun 21 - Jul 22	SUN 26	MON 27	TUE 28	WED 29	THU 1	FRI 2	SAT 3
	1A	1B	1A	1B	1AA	1AA	1B
	2A	2B	2A	2A	2AA	2A	2B
	3B	3A	3B	3A	3AA	3A	3A

LEO Jul 23 - Aug 22	SUN 26	MON 27	TUE 28	WED 29	THU 1	FRI 2	SAT 3
	1A	1B	1BB	1A	1B	1A	1A
	2B	2B	2B	2A	2B	2A	2A
	3B	3B	3B	3A	3A	3A	3A

VIRGO Aug 23 - Sep 22	SUN 26	MON 27	TUE 28	WED 29	THU 1	FRI 2	SAT 3
	1AA	1A	1B	1A	1A	1B	1B
	2AA	2A	2B	2AA	2A	2B	2B
	3A	3A	3B	3AA	3B	3B	3B

LIBRA Sep 23 - Oct 22	SUN 26	MON 27	TUE 28	WED 29	THU 1	FRI 2	SAT 3
	1A	1A	1B	1A	1A	1B	1BB
	2A	2A	2B	2A	2B	2B	2BB
	3A	3B	3A	3A	3B	3BB	3B

SCORPIO Oct 23 - Nov 22	SUN 26	MON 27	TUE 28	WED 29	THU 1	FRI 2	SAT 3
	1A	1B	1B	1A	1W	1A	1B
	2B	2A	2B	2A	2W	2B	2B
	3B	3B	3A	3AA	3A	3B	3A

SAGITTARIUS Nov 23 - Dec 21	SUN 26	MON 27	TUE 28	WED 29	THU 1	FRI 2	SAT 3
	1B	1A	1B	1A	1B	1BB	1A
	2B	2A	2A	2A	2B	2B	2B
	3B	3B	3A	3A	3BB	3A	3B

youR lucky staRs
March 4-10
1984

CAPRICORN δec 22 - jan 19	SUN 4	MON 5	TUE 6	WED 7	THU 8	FRI 9	SAT 10
	1 BB	1 A	1 B	1 A	1 B	1 BB	1 B
	2 B	2 A	2 B	2 A	2 B	2 BB	2 B
	3 B	3 A	3 A	3 B	3 B	3 B	3 B

AQUARIUS jan 20 - feb 19	SUN 4	MON 5	TUE 6	WED 7	THU 8	FRI 9	SAT 10
	1 A	1 B	1 AA	1 A	1 B	1 B	1 B
	2 A	2 A	2 AA	2 A	2 A	2 B	2 B
	3 B	3 A	3 A	3 B	3 A	3 B	3 B

PISCES feb 20 - mar 20	SUN 4	MON 5	TUE 6	WED 7	THU 8	FRI 9	SAT 10
	1 B	1 B	1 A	1 A	1 A	1 AA	1 B
	2 A	2 B	2 B	2 B	2 A	2 A	2 A
	3 B	3 A	3 B	3 A	3 AA	3 B	3 A

ARIES mar 21 - apr 19	SUN 4	MON 5	TUE 6	WED 7	THU 8	FRI 9	SAT 10
	1 A	1 B	1 B	1 BB	1 B	1 A	1 A
	2 B	2 A	2 B	2 BB	2 B	2 B	2 A
	3 B	3 A	3 BB	3 B	3 A	3 B	3 A

TAURUS apr 20 - may 20	SUN 4	MON 5	TUE 6	WED 7	THU 8	FRI 9	SAT 10
	1 A	1 AA	1 AA	1 A	1 B	1 BB	1 BB
	2 A	2 AA	2 A	2 B	2 B	2 BB	2 B
	3 A	3 AA	3 A	3 B	3 B	3 X	3 B

GEMINI may 21 - jun 20	SUN 4	MON 5	TUE 6	WED 7	THU 8	FRI 9	SAT 10
	1 B	1 A	1 A	1 AA	1 AA	1 A	1 B
	2 B	2 B	2 A	2 W	2 A	2 A	2 A
	3 A	3 B	3 A	3 AA	3 A	3 B	3 A

your Lucky stars
March 4-10
1984

CANCER Jun 21 - Jul 22	SUN 4	MON 5	TUE 6	WED 7	THU 8	FRI 9	SAT 10
	1 BB	1 B	1 B	1 A	1 B	1 BB	1 B
	2 BB	2 A	2 B	2 A	2 B	2 BB	2 A
	3 B	3 A	3 A	3 B	3 B	3 B	3 A

LEO Jul 23 - Aug 22	SUN 4	MON 5	TUE 6	WED 7	THU 8	FRI 9	SAT 10
	1 A	1 A	1 AA	1 B	1 A	1 B	1 B
	2 A	2 A	2 A	2 B	2 B	2 B	2 BB
	3 A	3 AA	3 B	3 A	3 B	3 A	3 X

VIRGO Aug 23 - Sep 22	SUN 4	MON 5	TUE 6	WED 7	THU 8	FRI 9	SAT 10
	1 A	1 A	1 B	1 B	1 BB	1 B	1 A
	2 B	2 A	2 A	2 B	2 BB	2 A	2 B
	3 B	3 B	3 A	3 B	3 B	3 A	3 B

LIBRA Sep 23 - Oct 22	SUN 4	MON 5	TUE 6	WED 7	THU 8	FRI 9	SAT 10
	1 B	1 A	1 AA	1 BB	1 X	1 B	1 B
	2 B	2 A	2 B	2 BB	2 X	2 B	2 B
	3 A	3 A	3 BB	3 X	3 BB	3 B	3 A

SCORPIO Oct 23 - Nov 22	SUN 4	MON 5	TUE 6	WED 7	THU 8	FRI 9	SAT 10
	1 AA	1 A	1 B	1 B	1 A	1 A	1 AA
	2 A	2 AA	2 B	2 A	2 B	2 A	2 AA
	3 A	3 A	3 B	3 A	3 B	3 A	3 A

SAGITTARIUS Nov 23 - Dec 21	SUN 4	MON 5	TUE 6	WED 7	THU 8	FRI 9	SAT 10
	1 A	1 B	1 A	1 B	1 A	1 B	1 A
	2 A	2 A	2 B	2 B	2 AA	2 B	2 B
	3 B	3 A	3 B	3 B	3 B	3 A	3 B

your lucky stars
March 11-17
1984

CAPRICORN	SUN 11	MON 12	TUE 13	WED 14	THU 15	FRI 16	SAT 17
DEC 22 - JAN 19	1 A	1 B	1 A	1 AA	1 A	1 A	1 B
	2 A	2 B	2 A	2 AA	2 A	2 A	2 B
	3 B	3 B	3 A	3 A	3 A	3 B	3 A

AQUARIUS	SUN 11	MON 12	TUE 13	WED 14	THU 15	FRI 16	SAT 17
JAN 20 - FEB 19	1 A	1 A	1 A	1 B	1 BB	1 A	1 B
	2 B	2 A	2 A	2 B	2 BB	2 A	2 B
	3 A	3 A	3 B	3 B	3 B	3 A	3 B

PISCES	SUN 11	MON 12	TUE 13	WED 14	THU 15	FRI 16	SAT 17
FEB 20 - MAR 20	1 B	1 B	1 B	1 B	1 A	1 A	1 A
	2 B	2 B	2 B	2 A	2 A	2 A	2 AA
	3 B	3 B	3 B	3 A	3 A	3 A	3 AA

ARIES	SUN 11	MON 12	TUE 13	WED 14	THU 15	FRI 16	SAT 17
MAR 21 - APR 19	1 B	1 A	1 A	1 A	1 A	1 A	1 A
	2 B	2 A	2 A	2 A	2 AA	2 A	2 A
	3 A	3 A	3 A	3 A	3 AA	3 A	3 B

TAURUS	SUN 11	MON 12	TUE 13	WED 14	THU 15	FRI 16	SAT 17
APR 20 - MAY 20	1 B	1 A	1 BB	1 B	1 B	1 A	1 A
	2 A	2 A	2 BB	2 B	2 A	2 A	2 A
	3 A	3 A	3 BB	3 B	3 A	3 A	3 A

GEMINI	SUN 11	MON 12	TUE 13	WED 14	THU 15	FRI 16	SAT 17
MAY 21 - JUN 20	1 A	1 B	1 A	1 A	1 B	1 BB	1 B
	2 B	2 B	2 A	2 A	2 B	2 BB	2 B
	3 B	3 A	3 A	3 A	3 BB	3 B	3 A

YOUR LUCKY STARS
March 11-17
1984

CANCER Jun 21 - Jul 22	SUN 11	MON 12	TUE 13	WED 14	THU 15	FRI 16	SAT 17
	1 BB	1 B	1 BB	1 B	1 B	1 AA	1 B
	2 BB	2 B	2 BB	2 B	2 A	2 W	2 B
	3 B	3 BB	3 BB	3 B	3 AA	3 A	3 B

LEO Jul 23 - Aug 22	SUN 11	MON 12	TUE 13	WED 14	THU 15	FRI 16	SAT 17
	1 A	1 A	1 A	1 AA	1 A	1 A	1 A
	2 A	2 A	2 A	2 AA	2 A	2 A	2 A
	3 A	3 A	3 AA	3 A	3 A	3 A	3 A

VIRGO Aug 23 · Sep 22	SUN 11	MON 12	TUE 13	WED 14	THU 15	FRI 16	SAT 17
	1 B	1 A	1 A	1 B	1 A	1 A	1 A
	2 B	2 A	2 B	2 B	2 A	2 A	2 B
	3 A	3 A	3 B	3 B	3 A	3 A	3 B

LIBRA Sep 23 - Oct 22	SUN 11	MON 12	TUE 13	WED 14	THU 15	FRI 16	SAT 17
	1 AA	1 A	1 B	1 B	1 B	1 B	1 BB
	2 A	2 B	2 B	2 B	2 B	2 B	2 BB
	3 A	3 B	3 B	3 B	3 B	3 BB	3 B

SCORPIO Oct 23 - Nov 22	SUN 11	MON 12	TUE 13	WED 14	THU 15	FRI 16	SAT 17
	1 A	1 B	1 B	1 B	1 A	1 A	1 A
	2 B	2 B	2 B	2 B	2 A	2 A	2 A
	3 B	3 B	3 B	3 B	3 A	3 A	3 A

SAGITTARIUS Nov 23 - Dec 21	SUN 11	MON 12	TUE 13	WED 14	THU 15	FRI 16	SAT 17
	1 B	1 B	1 B	1 A	1 AA	1 A	1 A
	2 A	2 B	2 B	2 A	2 AA	2 A	2 A
	3 B	3 B	3 A	3 A	3 A	3 A	3 B

your lucky stars

March 18-24
1984

CAPRICORN dec 22 - jan 19	SUN 18	MON 19	TUE 20	WED 21	THU 22	FRI 23	SAT 24
	1 A	1 B	1 A	1 B	1 B	1 A	1 AA
	2 A	2 B	2 A	2 B	2 B	2 A	2 A
	3 B	3 A	3 B	3 B	3 A	3 A	3 A

AQUARIUS jan 20 - feb 19	SUN 18	MON 19	TUE 20	WED 21	THU 22	FRI 23	SAT 24
	1 A	1 A	1 A	1 A	1 AA	1 A	1 A
	2 A	2 A	2 A	2 A	2 W	2 A	2 A
	3 A	3 A	3 A	3 AA	3 AA	3 A	3 B

PISCES feb 20 - mar 20	SUN 18	MON 19	TUE 20	WED 21	THU 22	FRI 23	SAT 24
	1 A	1 B	1 BB	1 BB	1 B	1 B	1 A
	2 B	2 BB	2 BB	2 BB	2 B	2 A	2 A
	3 B	3 BB	3 BB	3 BB	3 B	3 A	3 B

ARIES mar 21 - apr 19	SUN 18	MON 19	TUE 20	WED 21	THU 22	FRI 23	SAT 24
	1 B	1 A	1 AA	1 A	1 A	1 A	1 B
	2 B	2 A	2 AA	2 A	2 A	2 A	2 B
	3 A	3 A	3 A	3 A	3 A	3 B	3 B

TAURUS apr 20 - may 20	SUN 18	MON 19	TUE 20	WED 21	THU 22	FRI 23	SAT 24
	1 A	1 A	1 A	1 B	1 B	1 B	1 B
	2 A	2 A	2 A	2 B	2 B	2 B	2 A
	3 A	3 A	3 A	3 B	3 B	3 B	3 A

GEMINI may 21 - jun 20	SUN 18	MON 19	TUE 20	WED 21	THU 22	FRI 23	SAT 24
	1 A	1 B	1 A	1 A	1 A	1 A	1 A
	2 B	2 B	2 A	2 A	2 B	2 AA	2 A
	3 B	3 B	3 A	3 A	3 A	3 AA	3 B

YOUR LUCKY STARS
March 18-24
1984

CANCER
Jun 21 - Jul 22

	SUN 18	MON 19	TUE 20	WED 21	THU 22	FRI 23	SAT 24
1	A	B	A	A	A	B	BB
2	B	B	A	A	A	BB	B
3	B	A	A	A	A	BB	B

LEO
Jul 23 - Aug 22

	SUN 18	MON 19	TUE 20	WED 21	THU 22	FRI 23	SAT 24
1	B	A	B	B	BB	B	A
2	A	A	B	BB	BB	B	A
3	A	A	B	BB	B	A	A

VIRGO
Aug 23 - Sep 22

	SUN 18	MON 19	TUE 20	WED 21	THU 22	FRI 23	SAT 24
1	A	B	B	A	A	A	AA
2	A	B	A	A	A	A	AA
3	B	B	A	A	A	A	A

LIBRA
Sep 23 - Oct 22

	SUN 18	MON 19	TUE 20	WED 21	THU 22	FRI 23	SAT 24
1	A	B	A	B	B	A	AA
2	A	B	A	BB	A	A	A
3	B	A	B	B	A	A	A

SCORPIO
Oct 23 - Nov 22

	SUN 18	MON 19	TUE 20	WED 21	THU 22	FRI 23	SAT 24
1	B	A	A	AA	A	B	B
2	B	A	AA	A	A	B	B
3	A	A	AA	A	B	B	A

SAGITTARIUS
Nov 23 - Dec 21

	SUN 18	MON 19	TUE 20	WED 21	THU 22	FRI 23	SAT 24
1	B	B	BB	B	A	B	A
2	A	B	BB	B	A	B	A
3	B	B	B	B	B	A	B

your lucky stars
March 25-31
1984

CAPRICORN dec 22 - jan 19	SUN 25	MON 26	TUE 27	WED 28	THU 29	FRI 30	SAT 31
	1 B	1 AA	1 B	1 B	1 B	1 A	1 A
	2 A	2 A	2 B	2 B	2 B	2 A	2 B
	3 A	3 B	3 B	3 B	3 B	3 A	3 B

AQUARIUS jan 20 - feb 19	SUN 25	MON 26	TUE 27	WED 28	THU 29	FRI 30	SAT 31
	1 A	1 A	1 AA	1 A	1 A	1 A	1 B
	2 A	2 A	2 AA	2 B	2 A	2 B	2 B
	3 A	3 A	3 A	3 A	3 A	3 B	3 A

PISCES feb 20 - mar 20	SUN 25	MON 26	TUE 27	WED 28	THU 29	FRI 30	SAT 31
	1 A	1 A	1 BB	1 A	1 AA	1 A	1 A
	2 A	2 B	2 BB	2 A	2 AA	2 A	2 A
	3 A	3 BB	3 X	3 A	3 AA	3 A	3 A

ARIES mar 21 - apr 19	SUN 25	MON 26	TUE 27	WED 28	THU 29	FRI 30	SAT 31
	1 B	1 A	1 B	1 BB	1 X	1 B	1 BB
	2 B	2 A	2 B	2 BB	2 BB	2 B	2 B
	3 A	3 A	3 B	3 BB	3 BB	3 B	3 B

TAURUS apr 20 - may 20	SUN 25	MON 26	TUE 27	WED 28	THU 29	FRI 30	SAT 31
	1 A	1 B	1 A	1 B	1 A	1 BB	1 A
	2 A	2 B	2 A	2 A	2 B	2 BB	2 A
	3 A	3 B	3 B	3 A	3 B	3 B	3 B

GEMINI may 21 - jun 20	SUN 25	MON 26	TUE 27	WED 28	THU 29	FRI 30	SAT 31
	1 A	1 B	1 A	1 A	1 A	1 A	1 B
	2 A	2 B	2 A	2 AA	2 A	2 B	2 B
	3 B	3 A	3 A	3 AA	3 A	3 B	3 B

your lucky stars
March 25-31
1984

CANCER Jun 21 - Jul 22	SUN 25	MON 26	TUE 27	WED 28	THU 29	FRI 30	SAT 31
	1 A	1 B	1 BB	1 B	1 B	1 A	1 A
	2 A	2 B	2 BB	2 B	2 A	2 A	2 A
	3 A	3 B	3 BB	3 B	3 A	3 A	3 B

LEO Jul 23 - Aug 22	SUN 25	MON 26	TUE 27	WED 28	THU 29	FRI 30	SAT 31
	1 A	1 B	1 A	1 B	1 A	1 B	1 A
	2 B	2 B	2 A	2 B	2 A	2 B	2 A
	3 B	3 A	3 B	3 B	3 B	3 A	3 A

VIRGO Aug 23 - Sep 22	SUN 25	MON 26	TUE 27	WED 28	THU 29	FRI 30	SAT 31
	1 B	1 A	1 A	1 B	1 B	1 A	1 A
	2 A	2 A	2 B	2 B	2 A	2 AA	2 B
	3 A	3 A	3 B	3 B	3 A	3 A	3 B

LIBRA Sep 23 - Oct 22	SUN 25	MON 26	TUE 27	WED 28	THU 29	FRI 30	SAT 31
	1 AA	1 A	1 A	1 B	1 B	1 B	1 B
	2 A	2 A	2 A	2 B	2 B	2 B	2 A
	3 A	3 A	3 B	3 B	3 B	3 B	3 A

SCORPIO Oct 23 - Nov 22	SUN 25	MON 26	TUE 27	WED 28	THU 29	FRI 30	SAT 31
	1 AA	1 A	1 B	1 B	1 A	1 B	1 B
	2 AA	2 A	2 B	2 B	2 A	2 B	2 B
	3 A	3 A	3 B	3 A	3 A	3 B	3 A

SAGITTARIUS Nov 23 - Dec 21	SUN 25	MON 26	TUE 27	WED 28	THU 29	FRI 30	SAT 31
	1 B	1 B	1 B	1 A	1 A	1 A	1 A
	2 B	2 A	2 B	2 A	2 A	2 A	2 A
	3 B	3 A	3 A	3 A	3 A	3 A	3 B

your lucky stars
April 1-7
1984

CAPRICORN	SUN 1	MON 2	TUE 3	WED 4	THU 5	FRI 6	SAT 7
DEC 22 - JAN 19	1 B	1 B	1 B	1 A	1 A	1 AA	1 A
	2 B	2 B	2 B	2 A	2 A	2 A	2 A
	3 B	3 B	3 B	3 A	3 A	3 A	3 A

AQUARIUS	SUN 1	MON 2	TUE 3	WED 4	THU 5	FRI 6	SAT 7
JAN 20 - FEB 19	1 A	1 B	1 A	1 BB	1 BB	1 B	1 B
	2 A	2 A	2 B	2 BB	2 BB	2 B	2 B
	3 B	3 A	3 B	3 BB	3 BB	3 B	3 A

PISCES	SUN 1	MON 2	TUE 3	WED 4	THU 5	FRI 6	SAT 7
FEB 20 - MAR 20	1 A	1 B	1 A	1 B	1 B	1 B	1 B
	2 B	2 A	2 A	2 B	2 B	2 B	2 B
	3 B	3 A	3 B	3 B	3 B	3 A	3 A

ARIES	SUN 1	MON 2	TUE 3	WED 4	THU 5	FRI 6	SAT 7
MAR 21 - APR 19	1 AA	1 A	1 B	1 B	1 B	1 B	1 B
	2 AA	2 A	2 B	2 B	2 A	2 B	2 B
	3 AA	3 A	3 B	3 B	3 A	3 B	3 B

TAURUS	SUN 1	MON 2	TUE 3	WED 4	THU 5	FRI 6	SAT 7
APR 20 - MAY 20	1 A	1 B	1 A	1 B	1 BB	1 B	1 B
	2 A	2 A	2 B	2 B	2 BB	2 BB	2 B
	3 A	3 A	3 B	3 BB	3 B	3 BB	3 A

GEMINI	SUN 1	MON 2	TUE 3	WED 4	THU 5	FRI 6	SAT 7
MAY 21 - JUN 20	1 A	1 A	1 A	1 A	1 B	1 X	1 A
	2 B	2 A	2 A	2 A	2 B	2 BB	2 B
	3 B	3 A	3 A	3 A	3 BB	3 B	3 A

YOUR LUCKY STARS
April 1-7
1984

CANCER jun 21 - jul 22	SUN 1	MON 2	TUE 3	WED 4	THU 5	FRI 6	SAT 7
	1 A	1 A	1 A	1 A	1 A	1 AA	1 AA
	2 A	2 A	2 A	2 A	2 A	2 AA	2 AA
	3 A	3 A	3 A	3 A	3 A	3 AA	3 AA

LEO jul 23 - aug 22	SUN 1	MON 2	TUE 3	WED 4	THU 5	FRI 6	SAT 7
	1 B	1 B	1 BB	1 B	1 B	1 B	1 B
	2 B	2 B	2 BB	2 B	2 B	2 B	2 B
	3 BB	3 BB	3 BB	3 B	3 B	3 B	3 B

VIRGO aug 23 - sep 22	SUN 1	MON 2	TUE 3	WED 4	THU 5	FRI 6	SAT 7
	1 B	1 A	1 A	1 A	1 A	1 B	1 A
	2 B	2 A	2 A	2 A	2 A	2 B	2 A
	3 A	3 A	3 A	3 A	3 B	3 A	3 B

LIBRA sep 23 - oct 22	SUN 1	MON 2	TUE 3	WED 4	THU 5	FRI 6	SAT 7
	1 B	1 A	1 B	1 BB	1 A	1 A	1 B
	2 B	2 A	2 B	2 B	2 A	2 B	2 B
	3 A	3 B	3 BB	3 B	3 A	3 B	3 A

SCORPIO oct 23 - nov 22	SUN 1	MON 2	TUE 3	WED 4	THU 5	FRI 6	SAT 7
	1 A	1 A	1 A	1 B	1 B	1 B	1 A
	2 A	2 B	2 A	2 B	2 BB	2 B	2 B
	3 A	3 B	3 A	3 B	3 B	3 B	3 B

SAGITTARIUS nov 23 - dec 21	SUN 1	MON 2	TUE 3	WED 4	THU 5	FRI 6	SAT 7
	1 A	1 AA	1 B	1 B	1 A	1 B	1 BB
	2 A	2 AA	2 B	2 B	2 A	2 B	2 B
	3 AA	3 A	3 B	3 B	3 B	3 BB	3 A

YOUR LUCKY STARS
April 8-14
1984

	SUN 8	MON 9	TUE 10	WED 11	THU 12	FRI 13	SAT 14
CAPRICORN dec 22 - jan 19	1 X 2 X 3 X	1 X 2 BB 3 BB	1 BB 2 BB 3 B	1 B 2 B 3 B	1 B 2 B 3 A	1 A 2 A 3 B	1 B 2 B 3 A
	SUN 8	MON 9	TUE 10	WED 11	THU 12	FRI 13	SAT 14
aquarius jan 20 - feb 19	1 A 2 A 3 A	1 A 2 A 3 A	1 A 2 AA 3 A	1 A 2 A 3 B	1 A 2 A 3 A	1 A 2 A 3 A	1 A 2 A 3 B
	SUN 8	MON 9	TUE 10	WED 11	THU 12	FRI 13	SAT 14
pisces feb 20 - mar 20	1 A 2 A 3 B	1 B 2 B 3 B	1 BB 2 BB 3 BB	1 B 2 B 3 B	1 B 2 A 3 A	1 A 2 A 3 A	1 A 2 B 3 A
	SUN 8	MON 9	TUE 10	WED 11	THU 12	FRI 13	SAT 14
aries mar 21 - apr 19	1 A 2 A 3 A	1 A 2 A 3 A	1 A 2 AA 3 AA	1 A 2 A 3 A	1 A 2 B 3 B	1 B 2 B 3 B	1 B 2 A 3 A
	SUN 8	MON 9	TUE 10	WED 11	THU 12	FRI 13	SAT 14
taurus apr 20 - may 20	1 A 2 B 3 B	1 B 2 A 3 A	1 A 2 A 3 AA	1 A 2 A 3 AA	1 AA 2 AA 3 W	1 A 2 A 3 A	1 A 2 A 3 A
	SUN 8	MON 9	TUE 10	WED 11	THU 12	FRI 13	SAT 14
gemini may 21 - jun 20	1 B 2 B 3 B	1 A 2 A 3 A	1 A 2 A 3 A	1 A 2 A 3 A	1 A 2 A 3 B	1 B 2 B 3 B	1 BB 2 BB 3 BB

your lucky stars
April 8-14
1984

CANCER Jun 21 - Jul 22	SUN 8	MON 9	TUE 10	WED 11	THU 12	FRI 13	SAT 14
	1 B	1 A	1 A	1 A	1 B	1 B	1 B
	2 B	2 B	2 A	2 A	2 BB	2 B	2 B
	3 A	3 B	3 A	3 B	3 BB	3 B	3 B

LEO Jul 23 - Aug 22	SUN 8	MON 9	TUE 10	WED 11	THU 12	FRI 13	SAT 14
	1 A	1 A	1 B	1 A	1 AA	1 AA	1 A
	2 A	2 B	2 B	2 AA	2 W	2 A	2 A
	3 A	3 B	3 B	3 AA	3 W	3 A	3 A

VIRGO Aug 23 - Sep 22	SUN 8	MON 9	TUE 10	WED 11	THU 12	FRI 13	SAT 14
	1 A	1 B	1 B	1 A	1 B	1 B	1 A
	2 B	2 B	2 B	2 A	2 B	2 A	2 B
	3 B	3 B	3 A	3 A	3 B	3 A	3 A

LIBRA Sep 23 - Oct 22	SUN 8	MON 9	TUE 10	WED 11	THU 12	FRI 13	SAT 14
	1 A	1 B	1 A	1 AA	1 A	1 B	1 B
	2 A	2 B	2 A	2 A	2 A	2 B	2 A
	3 B	3 A	3 AA	3 A	3 A	3 B	3 B

SCORPIO Oct 23 - Nov 22	SUN 8	MON 9	TUE 10	WED 11	THU 12	FRI 13	SAT 14
	1 B	1 B	1 A	1 B	1 B	1 A	1 B
	2 B	2 A	2 A	2 B	2 A	2 A	2 B
	3 B	3 B	3 B	3 B	3 A	3 B	3 A

SAGITTARIUS Nov 23 - Dec 21	SUN 8	MON 9	TUE 10	WED 11	THU 12	FRI 13	SAT 14
	1 B	1 B	1 B	1 A	1 AA	1 AA	1 A
	2 A	2 B	2 A	2 A	2 AA	2 A	2 B
	3 A	3 B	3 A	3 AA	3 W	3 A	3 B

YOUR LUCKY STARS

April 15-21

1984

CAPRICORN dec 22 - jan 19	SUN 15	MON 16	TUE 17	WED 18	THU 19	FRI 20	SAT 21
	1A	1A	1A	1A	1A	1B	1B
	2A	2A	2A	2A	2A	2B	2A
	3A	3A	3A	3A	3B	3B	3A

AQUARIUS jan 20 - feb 19	SUN 15	MON 16	TUE 17	WED 18	THU 19	FRI 20	SAT 21
	1A	1A	1A	1A	1AA	1AA	1A
	2A	2A	2A	2A	2W	2A	2B
	3A	3A	3A	3AA	3AA	3A	3B

PISCES feb 20 - mar 20	SUN 15	MON 16	TUE 17	WED 18	THU 19	FRI 20	SAT 21
	1A	1A	1A	1BB	1BB	1B	1B
	2A	2A	2A	2BB	2B	2B	2B
	3AA	3A	3B	3BB	3B	3B	3B

ARIES mar 21 - apr 19	SUN 15	MON 16	TUE 17	WED 18	THU 19	FRI 20	SAT 21
	1A	1B	1A	1A	1B	1B	1A
	2A	2B	2A	2A	2BB	2B	2B
	3B	3A	3A	3A	3BB	3A	3A

TAURUS apr 20 - may 20	SUN 15	MON 16	TUE 17	WED 18	THU 19	FRI 20	SAT 21
	1B	1A	1A	1A	1A	1B	1B
	2B	2A⁻	2B	2A	2B	2B	2A
	3A	3A	3B	3A	3B	3B	3B

GEMINI may 21 - jun 20	SUN 15	MON 16	TUE 17	WED 18	THU 19	FRI 20	SAT 21
	1A	1A	1A	1A	1A	1B	1B
	2A	2A	2A	2A	2BB	2B	2B
	3A	3A	3A	3A	3BB	3B	3A

YOUR LUCKY STARS
April 15-21
1984

	SUN 15	MON 16	TUE 17	WED 18	THU 19	FRI 20	SAT 21
CANCER Jun 21 - Jul 22	1 B 2 A 3 A	1 A 2 A 3 A	1 A 2 A 3 A	1 A 2 AA 3 AA	1 A 2 A 3 A	1 A 2 B 3 B	1 B 2 B 3 A
LEO Jul 23 - Aug 22	1 B 2 B 3 B	1 A 2 A 3 A	1 A 2 B 3 B	1 B 2 B 3 B	1 B 2 A 3 A	1 A 2 A 3 A	1 A 2 A 3 A
VIRGO Aug 23 - Sep 22	1 A 2 A 3 B	1 B 2 B 3 B	1 B 2 B 3 B	1 B 2 B 3 B	1 A 2 A 3 A	1 A 2 A 3 A	1 A 2 B 3 B
LIBRA Sep 23 - Oct 22	1 A 2 B 3 A	1 A 2 A 3 A	1 A 2 A 3 A	1 A 2 A 3 A	1 B 2 BB 3 X	1 B 2 B 3 B	1 B 2 B 3 A
SCORPIO Oct 23 - Nov 22	1 A 2 A 3 A	1 A 2 A 3 A	1 B 2 B 3 B	1 BB 2 BB 3 X	1 B 2 B 3 B	1 B 2 A 3 A	1 A 2 B 3 A
SAGITTARIUS Nov 23 - Dec 21	1 B 2 B 3 A	1 A 2 A 3 A	1 A 2 A 3 A	1 B 2 B 3 B	1 B 2 B 3 B	1 B 2 B 3 B	1 B 2 B 3 B

43

YOUR LUCKY STARS
April 22-28
1984

CAPRICORN
dec 22 - jan 19

	SUN 22	MON 23	TUE 24	WED 25	THU 26	FRI 27	SAT 28
1	B	A	A	A	B	A	A
2	A	B	A	A	B	A	A
3	A	B	B	A	A	A	B

AQUARIUS
jan 20 - feb 19

	SUN 23	MON 24	TUE 25	WED 26	THU 27	FRI 28	SAT 29
1	A	B	B	A	A	B	B
2	A	B	A	AA	A	B	B
3	B	B	A	A	A	B	B

PISCES
feb 20 - mar 20

	SUN 22	MON 23	TUE 24	WED 25	THU 26	FRI 27	SAT 28
1	B	A	A	A	B	B	A
2	B	A	A	A	B	A	AA
3	A	A	A	A	B	A	AA

ARIES
mar 21 - apr 19

	SUN 22	MON 23	TUE 24	WED 25	THU 26	FRI 27	SAT 28
1	B	B	A	B	B	BB	B
2	A	B	A	B	B	BB	B
3	B	A	B	B	B	BB	A

TAURUS
apr 20 - may 20

	SUN 22	MON 23	TUE 24	WED 25	THU 26	FRI 27	SAT 28
1	A	B	A	B	A	A	B
2	B	A	A	BB	A	B	A
3	B	A	A	B	A	B	A

GEMINI
may 21 - jun 20

	SUN 22	MON 23	TUE 24	WED 25	THU 26	FRI 27	SAT 28
1	A	B	B	B	A	AA	A
2	A	B	A	B	A	A	B
3	A	B	B	B	A	A	B

YOUR LUCKY STARS
April 22-28
1984

	SUN 22	MON 23	TUE 24	WED 25	THU 26	FRI 27	SAT 28
CANCER Jun 21 - Jul 22	1 B 2 B 3 B	1 B 2 B 3 B	1 B 2 A 3 A	1 A 2 A 3 A	1 A 2 A 3 A	1 A 2 AA 3 A	1 A 2 AA 3 AA
	SUN 22	MON 23	TUE 24	WED 25	THU 26	FRI 27	SAT 28
LEO Jul 23 - Aug 22	1 A 2 B 3 B	1 B 2 B 3 B	1 B 2 B 3 B	1 A 2 A 3 A	1 A 2 A 3 B	1 B 2 B 3 B	1 B 2 B 3 A
	SUN 22	MON 23	TUE 24	WED 25	THU 26	FRI 27	SAT 28
VIRGO Aug 23 - Sep 22	1 A 2 A 3 A	1 A 2 A 3 B	1 B 2 B 3 B	1 BB 2 BB 3 BB	1 A 2 A 3 A	1 AA 2 AA 3 A	1 A 2 A 3 A
	SUN 22	MON 23	TUE 24	WED 25	THU 26	FRI 27	SAT 28
LIBRA Sep 23 - Oct 22	1 A 2 A 3 B	1 B 2 B 3 B	1 A 2 A 3 A	1 A 2 A 3 A	1 A 2 A 3 B	1 B 2 B 3 B	1 B 2 B 3 B
	SUN 22	MON 23	TUE 24	WED 25	THU 26	FRI 27	SAT 28
SCORPIO Oct 23 - Nov 22	1 A 2 A 3 A	1 B 2 B 3 B	1 B 2 B 3 B	1 A 2 A 3 AA	1 AA 2 AA 3 AA	1 A 2 A 3 A	1 A 2 B 3 A
	SUN 22	MON 23	TUE 24	WED 25	THU 26	FRI 27	SAT 28
SAGITTARIUS Nov 23 - Dec 21	1 A 2 B 3 B	1 B 2 B 3 A	1 A 2 A 3 A	1 A 2 A 3 A	1 W 2 AA 3 AA	1 A 2 A 3 A	1 A 2 A 3 A

YOUR LUCKY STARS

April 29 - May 5
1984

CAPRICORN DEC 22 - JAN 19	SUN 29	MON 30	TUE 1	WED 2	THU 3	FRI 4	SAT 5
	1A	1B	1B	1A	1AA	1A	1B
	2B	2B	2A	2A	2AA	2A	2B
	3B	3B	3B	3A	3A	3B	3A

AQUARIUS JAN 20 - FEB 19	SUN 29	MON 30	TUE 1	WED 2	THU 3	FRI 4	SAT 5
	1A	1A	1A	1A	1B	1B	1B
	2B	2A	2B	2A	2B	2B	2A
	3B	3A	3A	3A	3A	3B	3A

PISCES FEB 20 - MAR 20	SUN 29	MON 30	TUE 1	WED 2	THU 3	FRI 4	SAT 5
	1A	1B	1B	1A	1A	1B	1B
	2B	2B	2A	2A	2A	2B	2A
	3B	3B	3A	3A	3B	3A	3B

ARIES MAR 21 - APR 19	SUN 29	MON 30	TUE 1	WED 2	THU 3	FRI 4	SAT 5
	1A	1AA	1A	1A	1B	1B	1A
	2A	2AA	2A	2A	2B	2B	2B
	3A	3W	3A	3A	3B	3B	3B

TAURUS APR 20 - MAY 20	SUN 29	MON 30	TUE 1	WED 2	THU 3	FRI 4	SAT 5
	1A	1B	1A	1A	1B	1BB	1B
	2A	2B	2A	2A	2B	2BB	2B
	3B	3B	3A	3B	3B	3BB	3A

GEMINI MAY 21 - JUN 20	SUN 29	MON 30	TUE 1	WED 2	THU 3	FRI 4	SAT 5
	1B	1A	1A	1A	1B	1A	1B
	2B	2B	2A	2B	2B	2A	2BB
	3A	3A	3A	3B	3B	3A	3X

YOUR LUCKY STARS

April 29 - May 5

1984

CANCER Jun 21 - Jul 22	SUN 29	MON 30	TUE 1	WED 2	THU 3	FRI 4	SAT 5
1	B	B	B	A	B	A	A
2	B	B	B	B	B	A	A
3	B	B	A	B	B	A	B

LEO Jul 23 - Aug 22	SUN 29	MON 30	TUE 1	WED 2	THU 3	FRI 4	SAT 5
1	A	B	A	A	A	A	B
2	B	B	A	AA	A	B	B
3	B	A	A	AA	A	B	B

VIRGO Aug 23 - Sep 22	SUN 29	MON 30	TUE 1	WED 2	THU 3	FRI 4	SAT 5
1	A	W	B	A	A	B	A
2	AA	A	B	A	A	A	B
3	AA	B	A	A	A	B	B

LIBRA Sep 23 - Oct 22	SUN 29	MON 30	TUE 1	WED 2	THU 3	FRI 4	SAT 5
1	A	B	A	B	A	A	BB
2	B	B	A	B	A	BB	BB
3	B	A	A	A	A	BB	X

SCORPIO Oct 23 - Nov 22	SUN 29	MON 30	TUE 1	WED 2	THU 3	FRI 4	SAT 5
1	A	B	A	A	A	A	B
2	A	B	A	A	A	A	B
3	A	B	A	A	A	B	A

SAGITTARIUS Nov 23 - Dec 21	SUN 29	MON 30	TUE 1	WED 2	THU 3	FRI 4	SAT 5
1	A	A	B	A	B	A	A
2	B	A	B	A	B	A	A
3	B	A	B	A	B	A	A

YOUR LUCKY STARS

May 6 - 12

1984

CAPRICORN DEC 22 - JAN 19	SUN 6	MON 7	TUE 8	WED 9	THU 10	FRI 11	SAT 12
	1A	1B	1B	1A	1AA	1A	1A
	2A	2B	2B	2A	2AA	2A	2A
	3B	3B	3A	3A	3A	3A	3A

AQUARIUS JAN 20 - FEB 19	SUN 6	MON 7	TUE 8	WED 9	THU 10	FRI 11	SAT 12
	1B	1BB	1BB	1BB	1B	1A	1A
	2B	2BB	2BB	2B	2A	2A	2A
	3B	3BB	3BB	3B	3A	3A	3B

PISCES FEB 20 - MAR 20	SUN 6	MON 7	TUE 8	WED 9	THU 10	FRI 11	SAT 12
	1B	1B	1B	1A	1AA	1A	1A
	2B	2B	2B	2A	2A	2A	2B
	3B	3B	3A	3AA	3A	3A	3B

ARIES MAR 21 - APR 19	SUN 6	MON 7	TUE 8	WED 9	THU 10	FRI 11	SAT 12
	1AA	1A	1A	1A	1A	1B	1B
	2AA	2A	2A	2A	2A	2B	2B
	3AA	3A	3A	3A	3A	3B	3B

TAURUS APR 20 - MAY 20	SUN 6	MON 7	TUE 8	WED 9	THU 10	FRI 11	SAT 12
	1A	1A	1AA	1A	1A	1B	1B
	2A	2A	2AA	2A	2A	2B	2A
	3A	3A	3A	3A	3A	3B	3B

GEMINI MAY 21 - JUN 20	SUN 6	MON 7	TUE 8	WED 9	THU 10	FRI 11	SAT 12
	1B	1B	1B	1B	1A	1A	1A
	2BB	2B	2B	2B	2AA	2A	2B
	3BB	3B	3B	3B	3A	3A	3A

48

YOUR LUCKY STARS
May 6 - 12
1984

CANCER Jun 21 - Jul 22	SUN 6	MON 7	TUE 8	WED 9	THU 10	FRI 11	SAT 12
	1 A 2 B 3 B	1 B 2 B 3 B	1 B 2 B 3 B	1 BB 2 BB 3 BB	1 A 2 A 3 A	1 A 2 A 3 A	1 A 2 A 3 AA

LEO Jul 23 - Aug 22	SUN 6	MON 7	TUE 8	WED 9	THU 10	FRI 11	SAT 12
	1 A 2 A 3 A	1 B 2 B 3 A	1 A 2 A 3 A	1 B 2 B 3 B	1 A 2 A 3 A	1 A 2 A 3 A	1 A 2 B 3 B

VIRGO Aug 23 - Sep 22	SUN 6	MON 7	TUE 8	WED 9	THU 10	FRI 11	SAT 12
	1 A 2 B 3 B	1 A 2 A 3 A	1 A 2 A 3 A	1 B 2 B 3 BB	1 B 2 B 3 B	1 B 2 B 3 B	1 B 2 A 3 A

LIBRA Sep 23 - Oct 22	SUN 6	MON 7	TUE 8	WED 9	THU 10	FRI 11	SAT 12
	1 A 2 A 3 B	1 B 2 B 3 A	1 A 2 A 3 A	1 A 2 A 3 B	1 B 2 B 3 B	1 BB 2 BB 3 B	1 B 2 B 3 B

SCORPIO Oct 23 - Nov 22	SUN 6	MON 7	TUE 8	WED 9	THU 10	FRI 11	SAT 12
	1 B 2 B 3 B	1 B 2 B 3 A	1 A 2 A 3 AA	1 AA 2 AA 3 A	1 A 2 A 3 A	1 A 2 A 3 A	1 A 2 B 3 A

SAGITTARIUS Nov 23 - Dec 21	SUN 6	MON 7	TUE 8	WED 9	THU 10	FRI 11	SAT 12
	1 A 2 A 3 B	1 B 2 B 3 A	1 A 2 A 3 A	1 A 2 A 3 A	1 B 2 B 3 B	1 BB 2 BB 3 BB	1 BB 2 BB 3 B

49

your lucky stars
May 13 - 19
1984

CAPRICORN dec 22 - jan 19	SUN 13	MON 14	TUE 15	WED 16	THU 17	FRI 18	SAT 19
	1A	1AA	1A	1A	1A	1A	1B
	2A	2AA	2A	2A	2A	2A	2B
	3A	3A	3A	3A	3A	3B	3B

AQUARIUS jan 20 - feb 19	SUN 13	MON 14	TUE 15	WED 16	THU 17	FRI 18	SAT 19
	1A	1A	1A	1A	1B	1B	1B
	2B	2A	2A	2A	2B	2B	2B
	3B	3A	3A	3B	3BB	3B	3A

PISCES feb 20 - mar 20	SUN 13	MON 14	TUE 15	WED 16	THU 17	FRI 18	SAT 19
	1B	1A	1A	1A	1AA	1A	1A
	2B	2A	2A	2A	2AA	2A	2A
	3B	3B	3A	3A	3W	3A	3B

ARIES mar 21 - apr 19	SUN 13	MON 14	TUE 15	WED 16	THU 17	FRI 18	SAT 19
	1A	1A	1A	1B	1A	1AA	1A
	2B	2A	2A	2A	2A	2AA	2A
	3A	3A	3B	3A	3A	3A	3A

TAURUS apr 20 - may 20	SUN 13	MON 14	TUE 15	WED 16	THU 17	FRI 18	SAT 19
	1A	1A	1A	1A	1B	1B	1B
	2A	2A	2A	2A	2B	2B	2A
	3A	3A	3A	3A	3B	3B	3A

GEMINI may 21 - jun 20	SUN 13	MON 14	TUE 15	WED 16	THU 17	FRI 18	SAT 19
	1A	1A	1A	1A	1A	1B	1A
	2B	2A	2A	2A	2A	2B	2B
	3B	3A	3A	3A	3B	3A	3A

YOUR LUCKY STARS

May 13 - 19

1984

CANCER Jun 21 - Jul 22	SUN 13	MON 14	TUE 15	WED 16	THU 17	FRI 18	SAT 19
	1 B	1 B	1 A	1 A	1 A	1 B	1 BB
	2 B	2 B	2 A	2 A	2 B	2 BB	2 BB
	3 B	3 A	3 A	3 A	3 B	3 BB	3 BB

LEO Jul 23 - Aug 22	SUN 13	MON 14	TUE 15	WED 16	THU 17	FRI 18	SAT 19
	1 A	1 A	1 A	1 A	1 B	1 BB	1 A
	2 AA	2 A	2 A	2 B	2 B	2 BB	2 A
	3 AA	3 A	3 A	3 B	3 B	3 X	3 B

VIRGO Aug 23 - Sep 22	SUN 13	MON 14	TUE 15	WED 16	THU 17	FRI 18	SAT 19
	1 A	1 B	1 A	1 A	1 B	1 A	1 B
	2 A	2 BB	2 A	2 A	2 B	2 A	2 B
	3 A	3 B	3 A	3 B	3 A	3 B	3 A

LIBRA Sep 23 - Oct 22	SUN 13	MON 14	TUE 15	WED 16	THU 17	FRI 18	SAT 19
	1A	1A	1B	1B	1B	1B	1A
	2A	2B	2B	2BB	2B	2A	2A
	3A	3B	3B	3BB	3B	3A	3A

SCORPIO Oct 23 - Nov 22	SUN 13	MON 14	TUE 15	WED 16	THU 17	FRI 18	SAT 19
	1A	1A	1B	1B	1A	1A	1AA
	2A	2A	2B	2B	2A	2A	2AA
	3A	3A	3B	3A	3A	3AA	3A

SAGITTARIUS Nov 23 - Dec 21	SUN 13	MON 14	TUE 15	WED 16	THU 17	FRI 18	SAT 19
	1 AA	1A	1A	1A	1B	1 B	1 A
	2 AA	2A	2A	2A	2BB	2 B	2 A
	3 A	3A	3A	3A	3BB	3 B	3 A

your lucky stars
May 20 - 26
1984

CAPRICORN DEC 22 - JAN 19	SUN 20	MON 21	TUE 22	WED 23	THU 24	FRI 25	SAT 26
	1A	1A	1A	1AA	1A	1B	1A
	2B	2A	2A	2AA	2B	2A	2A
	3A	3A	3A	3A	3B	3A	3A

AQUARIUS JAN 20 - FEB 19	SUN 20	MON 21	TUE 22	WED 23	THU 24	FRI 25	SAT 26
	1A	1B	1B	1B	1A	1A	1B
	2A	2B	2B	2B	2A	2A	2B
	3B	3B	3B	3B	3A	3B	3A

PISCES FEB 20 - MAR 20	SUN 20	MON 21	TUE 22	WED 23	THU 24	FRI 25	SAT 26
	1 BB	1BB	1BB	1A	1B	1B	1A
	2 BB	2BB	2B	2A	2B	2B	2A
	3 BB	3BB	3B	3A	3A	3A	3B

ARIES MAR 21 - APR 19	SUN 20	MON 21	TUE 22	WED 23	THU 24	FRI 25	SAT 26
	1A	1A	1B	1B	1B	1B	1A
	2AA	2A	2B	2B	2B	2A	2A
	3AA	3A	3B	3B	3BB	3A	3AA

TAURUS APR 20 - MAY 20	SUN 20	MON 21	TUE 22	WED 23	THU 24	FRI 25	SAT 26
	1A	1B	1B	1B	1A	1A	1A
	2B	2B	2B	2A	2A	2A	2B
	3B	3B	3B	3A	3A	3A	3B

GEMINI MAY 21 - JUN 20	SUN 20	MON 21	TUE 22	WED 23	THU 24	FRI 25	SAT 26
	1A	1A	1AA	1A	1B	1B	1B
	2A	2AA	2A	2B	2B	2A	2B
	3A	3AA	3A	3B	3B	3A	3B

YOUR LUCKY STARS

May 20 - 26

1984

CANCER Jun 21 - Jul 22	SUN 20	MON 21	TUE 22	WED 23	THU 24	FRI 25	SAT 26
	1A	1A	1A	1A	1A	1B	1B
	2AA	2A	2A	2A	2A	2BB	2A
	3AA	3A	3A	3AA	3A	3B	3B

LEO Jul 23 - Aug 22	SUN 20	MON 21	TUE 22	WED 23	THU 24	FRI 25	SAT 26
	1A	1B	1B	1A	1A	1A	1A
	2A	2B	2B	2A	2B	2A	2B
	3B	3B	3A	3A	3B	3A	3A

VIRGO Aug 23 - Sep 22	SUN 20	MON 21	TUE 22	WED 23	THU 24	FRI 25	SAT 26
	1A	1B	1A	1A	1A	1A	1B
	2A	2B	2A	2AA	2A	2B	2B
	3B	3A	3A	3AA	3A	3B	3B

LIBRA Sep 23 - Oct 22	SUN 20	MON 21	TUE 22	WED 23	THU 24	FRI 25	SAT 26
	1B	1A	1B	1A	1B	1A	1A
	2B	2A	2B	2A	2B	2A	2AA
	3A	3A	3B	3B	3B	3A	3AA

SCORPIO Oct 23 - Nov 22	SUN 20	MON 21	TUE 22	WED 23	THU 24	FRI 25	SAT 26
	1B	1A	1A	1B	1B	1A	1B
	2BB	2A	2B	2B	2B	2A	2B
	3B	3A	3B	3B	3B	3A	3A

SAGITTARIUS Nov 23 - Dec 21	SUN 20	MON 21	TUE 22	WED 23	THU 24	FRI 25	SAT 26
	1B	1B	1A	1AA	1W	1A	1A
	2B	2B	2A	2AA	2AA	2A	2A
	3B	3A	3A	3AA	3AA	3A	3B

YOUR LUCKY STARS

May 27 - June 2

1984

CAPRICORN DEC 22 - JAN 19	SUN 27	MON 28	TUE 29	WED 30	THU 31	FRI 1	SAT 2
	1A	1B	1A	1A	1AA	1A	1A
	2B	2B	2A	2A	2AA	2A	2A
	3B	3A	3A	3AA	3W	3A	3A

AQUARIUS JAN 20 - FEB 19	SUN 27	MON 28	TUE 29	WED 30	THU 31	FRI 1	SAT 2
	1A	1A	1A	1B	1B	1A	1A
	2A	2A	2B	2BB	2B	2A	2B
	3A	3A	3B	3BB	3B	3A	3A

PISCES FEB 20 - MAR 20	SUN 27	MON 28	TUE 29	WED 30	THU 31	FRI 1	SAT 2
	1A	1A	1AA	1B	1B	1A	1B
	2A	2AA	2A	2B	2A	2A	2B
	3A	3AA	3A	3B	3A	3B	3B

ARIES MAR 21 - APR 19	SUN 27	MON 28	TUE 29	WED 30	THU 31	FRI 1	SAT 2
	1A	1B	1B	1A	1A	1A	1A
	2A	2B	2S	2B	2A	2A	2A
	3B	3B	3A	3B	3AA	3A	3B

TAURUS APR 20 - MAY 20	SUN 27	MON 28	TUE 29	WED 30	THU 31	FRI 1	SAT 2
	1B	1A	1A	1B	1A	1A	1A
	2B	2B	2B	2B	2A	2B	2B
	3A	3A	3B	3B	3A	3B	3B

GEMINI MAY 21 - JUN 20	SUN 27	MON 28	TUE 29	WED 30	THU 31	FRI 1	SAT 2
	1B	1B	1B	1B	1AA	1AA	1A
	2B	2B	2B	2A	2AA	2W	2A
	3B	3B	3B	3AA	3AA	3AA	3A

your lucky stars

May 27 - June 2

1984

CANCER
Jun 21 - Jul 22

	SUN 27	MON 28	TUE 29	WED 30	THU 31	FRI 1	SAT 2
1	A	B	A	A	B	A	A
2	A	B	A	A	B	A	A
3	B	B	A	BB	B	A	A

LEO
Jul 23 - Aug 22

	SUN 27	MON 28	TUE 29	WED 30	THU 31	FRI 1	SAT 2
1	A	B	B	B	A	A	B
2	A	B	BB	B	A	B	A
3	B	B	BB	A	A	B	B

VIRGO
Aug 23 - Sep 22

	SUN 27	MON 28	TUE 29	WED 30	THU 31	FRI 1	SAT 2
1	B	A	A	AA	B	B	A
2	B	A	A	A	B	B	A
3	A	A	AA	A	B	A	B

LIBRA
Sep 23 - Oct 22

	SUN 27	MON 28	TUE 29	WED 30	THU 31	FRI 1	SAT 2
1	A	A	A	AA	A	AA	B
2	B	A	A	W	A	AA	B
3	A	A	A	A	AA	A	B

SCORPIO
Oct 23 - Nov 22

	SUN 27	MON 28	TUE 29	WED 30	THU 31	FRI 1	SAT 2
1	A	A	AA	A	B	A	A
2	A	A	AA	B	B	A	B
3	A	A	AA	B	A	A	B

SAGITTARIUS
Nov 23 - Dec 21

	SUN 27	MON 28	TUE 29	WED 30	THU 31	FRI 1	SAT 2
1	B	A	A	A	A	B	B
2	B	A	A	AA	A	B	A
3	A	A	A	AA	A	B	A

55

YOUR LUCKY STARS

June 3 - 9

1984

CAPRICORN dec 22 - Jan 19	SUN 3	MON 4	TUE 5	WED 6	THU 7	FRI 8	SAT 9
	1B	1B	1A	1B	1A	1AA	1A
	2B	2A	2B	2B	2AA	2A	2A
	3B	3A	3B	3B	3AA	3A	3A

AQUARIUS Jan 20 - feb 19	SUN 3	MON 4	TUE 5	WED 6	THU 7	FRI 8	SAT 9
	1A	1A	1B	1B	1A	1A	1B
	2A	2B	2B	2B	2A	2A	2A
	3A	3B	3B	3B	3A	3A	3A

PISCES feb 20 - mar 20	SUN 3	MON 4	TUE 5	WED 6	THU 7	FRI 8	SAT 9
	1A	1A	1B	1AA	1AA	1B	1B
	2A	2A	2A	2AA	2AA	2B	2A
	3A	3B	3A	3W	3A	3B	3B

ARIES mar 21 - apr 19	SUN 3	MON 4	TUE 5	WED 6	THU 7	FRI 8	SAT 9
	1A	1A	1A	1A	1A	1B	1A
	2B	2A	2A	2A	2B	2B	2B
	3B	3A	3A	3A	3B	3A	3B

TAURUS apr 20 - may 20	SUN 3	MON 4	TUE 5	WED 6	THU 7	FRI 8	SAT 9
	1A	1B	1A	1B	1B	1A	1AA
	2A	2B	2A	2B	2B	2A	2AA
	3B	3A	3B	3B	3A	3A	3A

GEMINI may 21 - Jun 20	SUN 3	MON 4	TUE 5	WED 6	THU 7	FRI 8	SAT 9
	1B	1B	1BB	1BB	1B	1B	1A
	2A	2B	2BB	2BB	2B	2A	2A
	3B	3B	3BB	3BB	3B	3A	3A

YOUR LUCKY STARS

June 3 - 9

1984

CANCER Jun 21 - Jul 22	SUN 3	MON 4	TUE 5	WED 6	THU 7	FRI 8	SAT 9
	1 B	1 B	1 A	1 A	1 BB	1 B	1 A
	2 B	2 A	2 A	2 B	2 BB	2 A	2 A
	3 B	3 A	3 A	3 B	3 BB	3 A	3 B

LEO Jul 23 - Aug 22	SUN 3	MON 4	TUE 5	WED 6	THU 7	FRI 8	SAT 9
	1 A	1 B	1 B	1 A	1 A	1 AA	1 B
	2 A	2 B	2 B	2 A	2 A	2 AA	2 A
	3 B	3 B	3 B	3 A	3 A	3 A	3 B

VIRGO Aug 23 - Sep 22	SUN 3	MON 4	TUE 5	WED 6	THU 7	FRI 8	SAT 9
	1 B	1 A	1 A	1 B	1 BB	1 BB	1 A
	2 B	2 A	2 B	2 B	2 BB	2 A	2 B
	3 A	3 A	3 B	3 BB	3 X	3 A	3 B

LIBRA Sep 23 - Oct 22	SUN 3	MON 4	TUE 5	WED 6	THU 7	FRI 8	SAT 9
	1 B	1 B	1 B	1 B	1 A	1 A	1 A
	2 A	2 B	2 BB	2 B	2 A	2 AA	2 A
	3 B	3 B	3 BB	3 B	3 A	3 A	3 A

SCORPIO Oct 23 - Nov 22	SUN 3	MON 4	TUE 5	WED 6	THU 7	FRI 8	SAT 9
	1 A	1 A	1 B	1 B	1 B	1 A	1 B
	2 A	2 A	2 B	2 B	2 A	2 A	2 B
	3 A	3 A	3 B	3 B	3 A	3 A	3 A

SAGITTARIUS Nov 23 - Dec 21	SUN 3	MON 4	TUE 5	WED 6	THU 7	FRI 8	SAT 9
	1 A	1 B	1 B	1 A	1 AA	1 AA	1 B
	2 B	2 B	2 B	2 A	2 AA	2 A	2 B
	3 B	3 B	3 A	3 A	3 AA	3 B	3 B

YOUR LUCKY STARS

June 10 - 16
1984

CAPRICORN dec 22 - jan 19	SUN 10	MON 11	TUE 12	WED 13	THU 14	FRI 15	SAT 16
	1A	1A	1A	1B	1A	1B	1B
	2A	2B	2AA	2B	2A	2B	2A
	3A	3A	3A	3B	3B	3B	3A

AQUARIUS jan 20 - feb 19	SUN 10	MON 11	TUE 12	WED 13	THU 14	FRI 15	SAT 16
	1A	1B	1B	1A	1A	1AA	1B
	2B	2B	2A	2A	2A	2AA	2B
	3B	3B	3A	3A	3A	3A	3B

PISCES feb 20 - mar 20	SUN 10	MON 11	TUE 12	WED 13	THU 14	FRI 15	SAT 16
	1B	1B	1B	1B	1A	1A	1A
	2B	2B	2B	2B	2AA	2AA	2A
	3B	3A	3A	3A	3AA	3A	3B

ARIES mar 21 - apr 19	SUN 10	MON 11	TUE 12	WED 13	THU 14	FRI 15	SAT 16
	1A	1B	1BB	1A	1B	1B	1A
	2B	2B	2BB	2A	2B	2B	2A
	3A	3BB	3B	3B	3B	3A	3B

TAURUS apr 20 - may 20	SUN 10	MON 11	TUE 12	WED 13	THU 14	FRI 15	SAT 16
	1B	1AA	1AA	1A	1A	1B	1A
	2B	2AA	2AA	2A	2B	2B	2A
	3A	3AA	3A	3A	3B	3A	3A

GEMINI may 21 - jun 20	SUN 10	MON 11	TUE 12	WED 13	THU 14	FRI 15	SAT 16
	1B	1B	1A	1A	1B	1B	1A
	2A	2B	2A	2A	2B	2B	2A
	3B	3A	3A	3A	3A	3A	3B

58

YOUR LUCKY STARS

June 10 - 16

1984

CANCER Jun 21 - Jul 22	SUN 10	MON 11	TUE 12	WED 13	THU 14	FRI 15	SAT 16
	1 B	1 A	1 B	1 A	1 AA	1 A	1 A
	2 A	2 B	2 B	2 A	2 AA	2 A	2 A
	3 A	3 B	3 A	3 A	3 A	3 A	3 A

LEO Jul 23 - Aug 22	SUN 10	MON 11	TUE 12	WED 13	THU 14	FRI 15	SAT 16
	1 A	1 B	1 B	1 B	1 AA	1 A	1 B
	2 B	2 B	2 B	2 A	2 AA	2 B	2 B
	3 B	3 B	3 B	3 AA	3 W	3 B	3 B

VIRGO Aug 23 - Sep 22	SUN 10	MON 11	TUE 12	WED 13	THU 14	FRI 15	SAT 16
	1 A	1 A	1 A	1 B	1 B	1 B	1 B
	2 A	2 A	2 A	2 B	2 B	2 B	2 A
	3 A	3 A	3 B	3 B	3 B	3 B	3 A

LIBRA Sep 23 - Oct 22	SUN 10	MON 11	TUE 12	WED 13	THU 14	FRI 15	SAT 16
	1 A	1 A	1 A	1 B	1 B	1 AA	1 A
	2 B	2 A	2 A	2 B	2 AA	2 A	2 A
	3 A	3 A	3 B	3 B	3 AA	3 A	3 B

SCORPIO Oct 23 - Nov 22	SUN 10	MON 11	TUE 12	WED 13	THU 14	FRI 15	SAT 16
	1 B	1 A	1 AA	1 A	1 B	1 A	1 B
	2 B	2 A	2 AA	2 B	2 B	2 A	2 B
	3 A	3 A	3 A	3 B	3 A	3 A	3 A

SAGITTARIUS Nov 23 - Dec 21	SUN 10	MON 11	TUE 12	WED 13	THU 14	FRI 15	SAT 16
	1 B	1 A	1 A	1 A	1 AA	1 A	1 A
	2 B	2 A	2 A	2 A	2 AA	2 A	2 A
	3 B	3 A	3 A	3 AA	3 AA	3 A	3 B

your lucky stars

June 17 - 23

1984

CAPRICORN dec 22 - jan 19	SUN 17	MON 18	TUE 19	WED 20	THU 21	FRI 22	SAT 23
	1B	1A	1B	1B	1B	1A	1AA
	2B	2B	2A	2B	2B	2A	2AA
	3A	3B	3A	3B	3A	3A	3AA

AQUARIUS jan 20 - feb 19	SUN 17	MON 18	TUE 19	WED 20	THU 21	FRI 22	SAT 23
	1A	1B	1A	1B	1B	1A	1A
	2B	2B	2A	2B	2B	2A	2B
	3B	3A	3A	3BB	3A	3A	3B

PISCES feb 20 - mar 20	SUN 17	MON 18	TUE 19	WED 20	THU 20	FRI 22	SAT 23
	1B	1B	1A	1A	1B	1B	1B
	2B	2B	2A	2A	2B	2B	2B
	3B	3A	3A	3B	3B	3B	3B

ARIES mar 21 - apr 19	SUN 17	MON 18	TUE 19	WED 20	THU 21	FRI 22	SAT 23
	1A	1A	1B	1B	1A	1B	1B
	2B	2A	2B	2A	2A	2B	2B
	3A	3A	3B	3A	3A	3B	3A

TAURUS apr 20 - may 20	SUN 17	MON 18	TUE 19	WED 20	THU 21	FRI 22	SAT 23
	1A	1B	1B	1A	1A	1A	1A
	2A	2A	2B	2A	2A	2AA	2B
	3B	3A	3B	3A	3A	3AA	3A

GEMINI may 21 - jun 20	SUN 17	MON 18	TUE 19	WED 20	THU 21	FRI 22	SAT 23
	1A	1B	1A	1A	1A	1AA	1A
	2B	2A	2A	2A	2AA	2AA	2A
	3B	3A	3A	3A	3AA	3AA	3A

60

YOUR LUCKY STARS

June 17 – 23

1984

	SUN 17	MON 18	TUE 19	WED 20	THU 21	FRI 22	SAT 23
CANCER Jun 21 - Jul 22	1B 2B 3A	1AA 2W 3AA	1AA 2AA 3W	1A 2A 3A	1A 2A 3B	1B 2B 3B	1A 2A 3B
	SUN 17	MON 18	TUE 19	WED 20	THU 21	FRI 22	SAT 23
LEO Jul 23 - Aug 22	1A 2A 3A	1A 2A 3A	1A 2A 3A	1AA 2AA 3AA	1AA 2AA 3A	1A 2B 3B	1A 2B 3B
	SUN 17	MON 18	TUE 19	WED 20	THU 21	FRI 22	SAT 23
VIRGO Aug 23 - Sep 22	1A 2B 3B	1B 2A 3A	1A 2B 3B	1B 2A 3A	1A 2B 3B	1B 2BB 3B	1B 2B 3B
	SUN 17	MON 18	TUE 19	WED 20	THU 21	FRI 22	SAT 23
LIBRA Sep 23 - Oct 22	1A 2A 3A	1AA 2AA 3AA	1AA 2AA 3A	1A 2A 3B	1B 2A 3A	1A 2B 3B	1B 2B 3A
	SUN 17	MON 18	TUE 19	WED 20	THU 21	FRI 22	SAT 23
SCORPIO Oct 23 - Nov 22	1A 2A 3B	1B 2B 3A	1A 2A 3A	1A 2A 3A	1A 2B 3B	1B 2B 3B	1B 2A 3B
	SUN 17	MON 18	TUE 19	WED 20	THU 21	FRI 22	SAT 23
SAGITTARIUS Nov 23 - Dec 21	1A 2B 3B	1B 2B 3B	1B 2A 3A	1A 2A 3A	1AA 2AA 3AA	1AA 2AA 3AA	1A 2A 3A

YOUR LUCKY STARS

June 24 - 30
1984

CAPRICORN	SUN 24	MON 25	TUE 26	WED 27	THU 28	FRI 29	SAT 30
DEC 22 - JAN 19	1A	1A	1A	1A	1AA	1W	1A
	2A	2A	2A	2AA	2W	2AA	2AA
	3A	3A	3A	3AA	3W	3A	3A

AQUARIUS	SUN 24	MON 25	TUE 26	WED 27	THU 28	FRI 29	SAT 30
JAN 20 - FEB 19	1B	1B	1B	1B	1A	1AA	1B
	2BB	2BB	2B	2B	2A	2AA	2B
	3B	3B	3B	3B	3AA	3A	3BB

PISCES	SUN 24	MON 25	TUE 26	WED 27	THU 28	FRI 29	SAT 30
FEB 20 - MAR 20	1B	1A	1B	1B	1A	1A	1B
	2B	2B	2X	2B	2A	2A	2B
	3A	3B	3X	3B	3A	3A	3A

ARIES	SUN 24	MON 25	TUE 26	WED 27	THU 28	FRI 29	SAT 30
MAR 21 - APR 19	1A	1A	1A	1B	1A	1B	1B
	2A	2A	2B	2A	2A	2B	2B
	3A	3A	3B	3A	3A	3B	3A

TAURUS	SUN 24	MON 25	TUE 26	WED 27	THU 28	FRI 29	SAT 30
APR 20 - MAY 20	1AA	1A	1A	1A	1B	1B	1A
	2AA	2A	2A	2A	2B	2B	2B
	3AA	3A	3A	3B	3B	3B	3B

GEMINI	SUN 24	MON 25	TUE 26	WED 27	THU 28	FRI 29	SAT 30
MAY 21 - JUN 20	1A	1A	1A	1AA	1AA	1A	1A
	2A	2B	2A	2AA	2A	2A	2A
	3A	3B	3A	3AA	3A	3A	3AA

your lucky stars
June 24 - 30

1984

CANCER Jun 21 - Jul 22	SUN 24	MON 25	TUE 26	WED 27	THU 28	FRI 29	SAT 30
	1 A	1 B	1 B	1 B	1 A	1 AA	1 AA
	2 B	2 A	2 B	2 B	2 A	2 AA	2 A
	3 B	3 A	3 B	3 A	3 AA	3 AA	3 A

LEO Jul 23 - Aug 22	SUN 24	MON 25	TUE 26	WED 27	THU 28	FRI 29	SAT 30
	1 B	1 B	1 A	1 B	1 B	1 B	1 B
	2 A	2 A	2 A	2 BB	2 A	2 B	2 A
	3 A	3 A	3 B	3 BB	3 A	3 A	3 B

VIRGO Aug 23 - Sep 22	SUN 24	MON 25	TUE 26	WED 27	THU 28	FRI 29	SAT 30
	1 A	1 BB	1 BB	1 A	1 AA	1 A	1 A
	2 A	2 BB	2 B	2 A	2 AA	2 A	2 A
	3 BB	3 X	3 A	3 A	3 A	3 A	3 A

LIBRA Sep 23 - Oct 22	SUN 24	MON 25	TUE 26	WED 27	THU 28	FRI 29	SAT 30
	1 B	1 B	1 A	1 B	1 A	1 B	1 A
	2 B	2 BB	2 A	2 B	2 AA	2 B	2 B
	3 B	3 B	3 B	3 B	3 AA	3 B	3 B

SCORPIO Oct 23 - Nov 22	SUN 24	MON 25	TUE 26	WED 27	THU 28	FRI 29	SAT 30
	1 A	1 A	1 B	1 A	1 AA	1 A	1 A
	2 A	2 A	2 B	2 A	2 AA	2 A	2 B
	3 A	3 B	3 A	3 A	3 AA	3 A	3 B

SAGITTARIUS Nov 23 - Dec 21	SUN 24	MON 25	TUE 26	WED 27	THU 28	FRI 29	SAT 30
	1 A	1 B	1 B	1 A	1 B	1 A	1 A
	2 B	2 B	2 A	2 A	2 B	2 A	2 A
	3 B	3 A	3 B	3 B	3 A	3 A	3 B

63

YOUR LUCKY STARS

July 1 - 7

1984

CAPRICORN DEC 22 - JAN 19	SUN 1	MON 2	TUE 3	WED 4	THU 5	FRI 6	SAT 7
	1 B	1 A	1 B	1 B	1 A	1 AA	1 A
	2 A	2 A	2 B	2 B	2 A	2 A	2 A
	3 A	3 B	3 B	3 A	3 AA	3 A	3 A

AQUARIUS JAN 20 - FEB 19	SUN 1	MON 2	TUE 3	WED 4	THU 5	FRI 6	SAT 7
	1 B	1 B	1 B	1 A	1 A	1 B	1 B
	2 B	2 B	2 B	2 A	2 B	2 A	2 B
	3 B	3 B	3 B	3 A	3 B	3 A	3 A

PISCES FEB 20 - MAR 20	SUN 1	MON 2	TUE 3	WED 4	THU 5	FRI 6	SAT 7
	1 A	1 A	1 A	1 B	1 B	1 A	1 A
	2 B	2 A	2 B	2 B	2 B	2 A	2 B
	3 B	3 A	3 B	3 B	3 B	3 A	3 B

ARIES MAR 21 - APR 19	SUN 1	MON 2	TUE 3	WED 4	THU 5	FRI 6	SAT 7
	1 A	1 B	1 B	1 B	1 A	1 B	1 B
	2 A	2 B	2 BB	2 A	2 A	2 B	2 B
	3 A	3 B	3 BB	3 A	3 B	3 B	3 B

TAURUS APR 20 - MAY 20	SUN 1	MON 2	TUE 3	WED 4	THU 5	FRI 6	SAT 7
	1 B	1 A	1 A	1 B	1 B	1 A	1 A
	2 B	2 A	2 B	2 B	2 B	2 A	2 B
	3 A	3 A	3 B	3 B	3 A	3 A	3 A

GEMINI MAY 21 - JUN 20	SUN 1	MON 2	TUE 3	WED 4	THU 5	FRI 6	SAT 7
	1 B	1 A	1 A	1 B	1 B	1 A	1 A
	2 A	2 AA	2 A	2 B	2 A	2 B	2 A
	3 A	3 AA	3 B	3 B	3 A	3 B	3 B

your lucky stars
July 1 - 7
1984

	SUN 1	MON 2	TUE 3	WED 4	THU 5	FRI 6	SAT 7
CANCER Jun 21 - Jul 22	1 B 2 B 3 B	1 B 2 B 3 B	1 B 2 A 3 A	1 A 2 A 3 A	1 A 2 A 3 A	1 AA 2 A 3 A	1 A 2 B 3 B
LEO Jul 23 - Aug 22	1 B 2 B 3 A	1 A 2 A 3 A	1 A 2 B 3 B	1 BB 2 BB 3 BB	1 BB 2 B 3 B	1 B 2 A 3 A	1 A 2 A 3 A
VIRGO Aug 23 - Sep 22	1 B 2 A 3 A	1 A 2 B 3 B	1 B 2 B 3 B	1 A 2 A 3 A	1 B 2 B 3 A	1 A 2 B 3 B	1 A 2 A 3 A
LIBRA Sep 23 - Oct 22	1 A 2 B 3 A	1 A 2 A 3 A	1 A 2 A 3 A	1 A 2 A 3 A	1 A 2 A 3 A	1 B 2 B 3 B	1 B 2 A 3 A
SCORPIO Oct 23 - Nov 22	1 A 2 A 3 A	1 A 2 A 3 B	1 B 2 B 3 B	1 A 2 A 3 A	1 A 2 A 3 A	1 AA 2 AA 3 A	1 A 2 A 3 B
SAGITTARIUS Nov 23 - Dec 21	1 A 2 A 3 B	1 B 2 B 3 A	1 A 2 A 3 A	1 A 2 A 3 A	1 A 2 A 3 B	1 B 2 B 3 B	1 B 2 B 3 B

YOUR LUCKY STARS
July 8 - 14
1984

CAPRICORN dec 22 - jan 19	SUN 8	MON 9	TUE 10	WED 11	THU 12	FRI 13	SAT 14
	1 A	1 A	1 B	1 A	1 B	1 B	1 A
	2 A	2 A	2 B	2 B	2 B	2 B	2 B
	3 A	3 A	3 A	3 B	3 B	3 A	3 B

AQUARIUS jan 20 - feb 19	SUN 8	MON 9	TUE 10	WED 11	THU 12	FRI 13	SAT 14
	1 B	1 A	1 A	1 A	1 B	1 A	1 A
	2 B	2 AA	2 A	2 B	2 B	2 A	2 B
	3 A	3 AA	3 A	3 B	3 A	3 A	3 B

PISCES feb 20 - mar 20	SUN 8	MON 9	TUE 10	WED 11	THU 12	FRI 13	SAT 14
	1 A	1 B	1 B	1 B	1 B	1 A	1 A
	2 A	2 B	2 B	2 B	2 A	2 A	2 A
	3 B	3 B	3 B	3 B	3 A	3 A	3 A

ARIES mar 21 - apr 19	SUN 8	MON 9	TUE 10	WED 11	THU 12	FRI 13	SAT 14
	1 B	1 A	1 B	1 A	1 A	1 AA	1 AA
	2 A	2 B	2 B	2 A	2 A	2 W	2 AA
	3 A	3 B	3 B	3 A	3 A	3 AA	3 AA

TAURUS apr 20 - may 20	SUN 8	MON 9	TUE 10	WED 11	THU 12	FRI 13	SAT 14
	1 A	1 A	1 A	1 A	1 A	1 B	1 A
	2 A	2 A	2 B	2 A	2 B	2 B	2 A
	3 A	3 A	3 B	3 A	3 B	3 A	3 B

GEMINI may 21 - jun 20	SUN 8	MON 9	TUE 10	WED 11	THU 12	FRI 13	SAT 14
	1 A	1 A	1 A	1 B	1 A	1 A	1 B
	2 A	2 A	2 A	2 B	2 A	2 A	2 B
	3 A	3 A	3 B	3 B	3 A	3 B	3 B

YOUR LUCKY STARS
July 8 - 14
1984

	SUN 8	MON 9	TUE 10	WED 11	THU 12	FRI 13	SAT 14
CANCER Jun 21 - Jul 22	1B 2A 3A	1B 2B 3B	1B 2B 3A	1A 2B 3B	1A 2A 3A	1A 2B 3B	1B 2A 3B
LEO Jul 23 - Aug 22	1B 2A 3A	1A 2A 3AA	1AA 2A 3A	1A 2B 3B	1B 2B 3B	1B 2A 3A	1A 2A 3A
VIRGO Aug 23 - Sep 22	1B 2B 3B	1B 2B 3B	1B 2B 3B	1B 2B 3A	1A 2A 3A	1A 2A 3A	1A 2A 3A
LIBRA Sep 23 - Oct 22	1B 2B 3A	1A 2A 3A	1A 2B 3B	1A 2A 3B	1B 2B 3B	1A 2A 3A	1A 2AA 3A
SCORPIO Oct 23 - Nov 22	1A 2A 3B	1B 2B 3B	1BB 2BB 3BB	1BB 2B 3B	1A 2A 3A	1A 2B 3B	1B 2A 3A
SAGITTARIUS Nov 23 - Dec 21	1B 2B 3A	1A 2B 3B	1B 2B 3A	1A 2A 3A	1A 2A 3A	1BB 2BB 3BB	1X 2BB 3BB

your lucky stars
July 15 - 21
1984

CAPRICORN dec 22 - jan 19	SUN 15	MON 16	TUE 17	WED 18	THU 19	FRI 20	SAT 21
	1A	1B	1B	1A	1B	1A	1A
	2A	2B	2B	2A	2B	2A	2A
	3B	3B	3A	3B	3A	3A	3A

AQUARIUS jan 20 - feb 19	SUN 15	MON 16	TUE 17	WED 18	THU 19	FRI 20	SAT 21
	1BB	1B	1B	1A	1A	1A	1A
	2BB	2B	2B	2A	2A	2A	2A
	3B	3B	3A	3A	3A	3A	3B

PISCES feb 20 - mar 20	SUN 15	MON 16	TUE 17	WED 18	THU 19	FRI 20	SAT 21
	1A	1B	1A	1B	1A	1B	1B
	2A	2A	2B	2B	2A	2B	2A
	3B	3A	3B	3A	3A	3B	3A

ARIES mar 21 - apr 19	SUN 15	MON 16	TUE 17	WED 18	THU 19	FRI 20	SAT 21
	1B	1B	1A	1B	1A	1AA	1A
	2A	2B	2A	2A	2A	2AA	2A
	3A	3B	3A	3A	3A	3AA	3B

TAURUS apr 20 - may 20	SUN 15	MON 16	TUE 17	WED 18	THU 19	FRI 20	SAT 21
	1B	1B	1A	1A	1B	1A	1AA
	2B	2B	2A	2B	2B	2A	2AA
	3B	3A	3A	3B	3A	3A	3A

GEMINI may 21 - jun 20	SUN 15	MON 16	TUE 17	WED 18	THU 19	FRI 20	SAT 21
	1A	1B	1B	1A	1A	1B	1B
	2B	2B	2A	2B	2A	2B	2A
	3B	3B	3A	3A	3B	3B	3A

YOUR LUCKY STARS
July 15 - 21
1984

	SUN 15	MON 16	TUE 17	WED 18	THU 19	FRI 20	SAT 21
CANCER Jun 21 - Jul 22	1A 2A 3B	1B 2B 3B	1B 2A 3A	1AA 2AA 3AA	1W 2W 3AA	1A 2A 3B	1B 2B 3B
LEO Jul 23 - Aug 22	1B 2B 3A	1B 2B 3A	1A 2A 3A	1B 2A 3B	1B 2B 3B	1B 2B 3A	1A 2A 3A
VIRGO Aug 23 - Sep 22	1B 2A 3B	1B 2A 3A	1A 2A 3AA	1AA 2W 3AA	1A 2A 3A	1A 2A 3B	1B 2B 3A
LIBRA Sep 23 - Oct 22	1B 2A 3A	1A 2A 3A	1A 2A 3B	1BB 2BB 3BB	1BB 2W 3BB	1B 2A 3A	1A 2A 3B
SCORPIO Oct 23 - Nov 22	1A 2A 3A	1A 2A 3A	1B 2B 3B	1B 2B 3B	1B 2B 3B	1BB 2BB 3B	1B 2A 3A
SAGITTARIUS Nov 23 - Dec 21	1A 2B 3B	1B 2B 3B	1B 2B 3A	1A 2A 3B	1B 2A 3A	1B 2B 3B	1B 2A 3A

69

your lucky stars

July 22 - 28
1984

CAPRICORN dec 22 - jan 19	SUN 22	MON 23	TUE 24	WED 25	THU 26	FRI 27	SAT 28
	1B	1B	1BB	1B	1A	1A	1B
	2B	2B	2BB	2A	2A	2B	2B
	3B	3B	3B	3A	3A	3B	3A

aquarius jan 20 - feb 19	SUN 22	MON 23	TUE 24	WED 25	THU 26	FRI 27	SAT 28
	1B	1A	1A	1AA	1B	1A	1B
	2A	2A	2A	2A	2B	2B	2B
	3A	3A	3A	3A	3B	3B	3B

pisces feb 20 - mar 20	SUN 22	MON 23	TUE 24	WED 25	THU 26	FRI 27	SAT 28
	1B	1B	1A	1A	1A	1B	1B
	2B	2B	2A	2A	2B	2B	2A
	3A	3B	3A	3A	3B	3B	3A

aries mar 21 - apr 19	SUN 22	MON 23	TUE 24	WED 25	THU 26	FRI 27	SAT 28
	1A	1A	1A	1AA	1A	1B	1A
	2A	2A	2A	2AA	2A	2B	2A
	3A	3A	3A	3AA	3B	3B	3B

taurus apr 20 - may 20	SUN 22	MON 23	TUE 24	WED 25	THU 26	FRI 27	SAT 28
	1A	1B	1A	1B	1A	1AA	1A
	2B	2B	2A	2B	2AA	2W	2B
	3B	3A	3B	3B	3AA	3AA	3B

Gemini may 21 - jun 20	SUN 22	MON 23	TUE 24	WED 25	THU 26	FRI 27	SAT 28
	1A	1B	1A	1B	1A	1B	1A
	2A	2B	2B	2B	2A	2B	2A
	3B	3B	3B	3A	3B	3A	3A

70

YOUR LUCKY STARS

July 22 - 28

1984

	SUN 22	MON 23	TUE 24	WED 25	THU 26	FRI 27	SAT 28
CANCER Jun 21 - Jul 22	1 B 2 A 3 A	1 A 2 A 3 AA	1 A 2 A 3 A	1 A 2 A 3 A	1 A 2 A 3 B	1 B 2 B 3 B	1 B 2 A 3 B
	SUN 22	MON 23	TUE 24	WED 25	THU 26	FRI 27	SAT 28
LEO Jul 23 - Aug 22	1A 2A 3B	1B 2B 3B	1BB 2BB 3BB	1BB 2B 3A	1A 2A 3AA	1AA 2AA 3AA	1A 2A 3A
	SUN 22	MON 23	TUE 24	WED 25	THU 26	FRI 27	SAT 28
VIRGO Aug 23 - Sep 22	1B 2B 3B	1B 2B 3B	1B 2B 3A	1A 2A 3A	1A 2A 3B	1B 2B 3B	1B 2A 3A
	SUN 22	MON 23	TUE 24	WED 25	THU 26	FRI 27	SAT 28
LIBRA Sep 23 - Oct 22	1A 2A 3A	1A 2A 3AA	1AA 2A 3A	1A 2A 3A	1A 2A 3B	1BB 2BB 3B	1B 2B 3A
	SUN 22	MON 23	TUE 24	WED 25	THU 26	FRI 27	SAT 28
SCORPIO Oct 23 - Nov 22	1A 2B 3B	1B 2B 3B	1B 2A 3A	1A 2B 3B	1A 2A 3A	1A 2A 3A	1A 2B 3B
	SUN 22	MON 23	TUE 24	WED 25	THU 26	FRI 27	SAT 28
SAGITTARIUS Nov 23 - Dec 21	1B 2B 3A	1B 2B 3A	1A 2A 3A	1B 2B 3B	1B 2B 3B	1B 2A 3A	1A 2A 3B

71

your lucky stars

July 29 - August 4
1984

CAPRICORN δεc 22 - jan 19	SUN 29	MON 30	TUE 31	WED 1	THU 2	FRI 3	SAT 4
	1 B	1 A	1 B	1 A	1 AA	1 A	1 B
	2 B	2 A	2 B	2 A	2 A	2 B	2 A
	3 A	3 A	3 B	3 A	3 A	3 B	3 B

AQUARIUS jan 20 - feb 19	SUN 29	MON 30	TUE 31	WED 1	THU 2	FRI 3	SAT 4
	1 B	1 A	1 A	1 B	1 B	1 A	1 A
	2 A	2 A	2 A	2 B	2 A	2 A	2 A
	3 A	3 A	3 A	3 B	3 A	3 A	3 B

PISCES feb 20 - mar 20	SUN 29	MON 30	TUE 31	WED 1	THU 2	FRI 3	SAT 4
	1 A	1 B	1 A	1 AA	1 AA	1 A	1 B
	2 B	2 B	2 A	2 AA	2 A	2 B	2 B
	3 B	3 A	3 A	3 AA	3 A	3 B	3 A

ARIES mar 21 - apr 19	SUN 29	MON 30	TUE 31	WED 1	THU 2	FRI 3	SAT 4
	1 A	1 A	1 B	1 B	1 A	1 A	1 B
	2 A	2 B	2 B	2 B	2 A	2 A	2 A
	3 A	3 B	3 B	3 B	3 A	3 A	3 A

TAURUS apr 20 - may 20	SUN 29	MON 30	TUE 31	WED 1	THU 2	FRI 3	SAT 4
	1 A	1 B	1 B	1 X	1 B	1 B	1 A
	2 A	2 B	2 B	2 X	2 B	2 B	2 B
	3 B	3 B	3 X	3 BB	3 B	3 A	3 A

GEMINI may 21 - jun 20	SUN 29	MON 30	TUE 31	WED 1	THU 2	FRI 3	SAT 4
	1 A	1 A	1 A	1 B	1 B	1 A	1 A
	2 A	2 AA	2 B	2 B	2 B	2 A	2 B
	3 A	3 AA	3 B	3 B	3 A	3 A	3 A

YOUR LUCKY STARS
July 29 - August 4
1984

CANCER Jun 21 - Jul 22	SUN 29	MON 30	TUE 31	WED 1	THU 2	FRI 3	SAT 4
	1B	1A	1B	1B	1B	1B	1A
	2B	2B	2A	2B	2A	2A	2A
	3A	3B	3A	3B	3A	3A	3B

LEO Jul 23 - Aug 22	SUN 29	MON 30	TUE 31	WED 1	THU 2	FRI 3	SAT 4
	1A	1A	1A	1A	1AA	1B	1A
	2A	2B	2A	2A	2AA	2B	2A
	3B	3B	3A	3A	3AA	3B	3B

VIRGO Aug 23 - Sep 22	SUN 29	MON 30	TUE 31	WED 1	THU 2	FRI 3	SAT 4
	1A	1B	1A	1AA	1W	1A	1B
	2B	2B	2A	2AA	2W	2A	2B
	3B	3A	3A	3AA	3A	3A	3A

LIBRA Sep 23 - Oct 22	SUN 29	MON 30	TUE 31	WED 1	THU 2	FRI 3	SAT 4
	1B	1B	1B	1BB	1BB	1B	1A
	2B	2B	2B	2BB	2BB	2B	2A
	3B	3B	3B	3BB	3BB	3A	3B

SCORPIO Oct 23 - Nov 22	SUN 29	MON 30	TUE 31	WED 1	THU 2	FRI 3	SAT 4
	1B	1B	1B	1A	1AA	1A	1A
	2A	2B	2A	2AA	2A	2W	2A
	3B	3B	3A	3AA	3A	3A	3A

SAGITTARIUS Nov 23 - Dec 21	SUN 29	MON 30	TUE 31	WED 1	THU 2	FRI 3	SAT 4
	1B	1A	1AA	1B	1A	1B	1B
	2A	2A	2AA	2B	2A	2B	2B
	3A	3A	3B	3B	3B	3B	3B

73

YOUR LUCKY STARS

August 5 - 11

1984

	SUN 5	MON 6	TUE 7	WED 8	THU 9	FRI 10	SAT 11
CAPRICORN dec 22 - jan 19	1 A 2 A 3 B	1 B 2 A 3 A	1 A 2 A 3 A	1 B 2 B 3 B	1 X 2 B 3 B	1 B 2 A 3 A	1 A 2 A 3 A
	SUN 5	**MON** 6	**TUE** 7	**WED** 8	**THU** 9	**FRI** 10	**SAT** 11
AQUARIUS jan 20 - feb 19	1 B 2 B 3 A	1 A 2 A 3 B	1 B 2 A 3 A	1 B 2 B 3 B	1 A 2 B 3 B	1 B 2 A 3 A	1 A 2 A 3 A
	SUN 5	**MON** 6	**TUE** 7	**WED** 8	**THU** 9	**FRI** 10	**SAT** 11
PISCES feb 20 - mar 20	1 A 2 A 3 B	1 A 2 A 3 B	1 B 2 B 3 B	1 BB 2 BB 3 BB	1 B 2 A 3 A	1 A 2 A 3 B	1 B 2 BB 3 BB
	SUN 5	**MON** 6	**TUE** 7	**WED** 8	**THU** 9	**FRI** 10	**SAT** 11
ARIES mar 21 - apr 19	1 A 2 A 3 A	1 A 2 AA 3 AA	1 W 2 A 3 A	1 A 2 A 3 B	1 B 2 B 3 BB	1 BB 2 B 3 A	1 A 2 A 3 A
	SUN 5	**MON** 6	**TUE** 7	**WED** 8	**THU** 9	**FRI** 10	**SAT** 11
TAURUS apr 20 - may 20	1 A 2 A 3 A	1 A 2 B 3 BB	1 BB 2 X 3 BB	1 BB 2 BB 3 BB	1 B 2 B 3 B	1 A 2 A 3 B	1 B 2 B 3 A
	SUN 5	**MON** 6	**TUE** 7	**WED** 8	**THU** 9	**FRI** 10	**SAT** 11
GEMINI may 21 - jun 20	1 B 2 A 3 B	1 B 2 B 3 B	1 B 2 A 3 A	1 A 2 AA 3 A	1 B 2 B 3 B	1 A 2 B 3 A	1 A 2 BB 3 BB

YOUR LUCKY STARS

August 5 - 11

1984

	SUN 5	MON 6	TUE 7	WED 8	THU 9	FRI 10	SAT 11
CANCER Jun 21 - Jul 22	1 B 2 B 3 B	1B 2A 3A	1A 2B 3B	1A 2A 3A	1A 2A 3B	1B 2B 3B	1A 2B 3B

	SUN 5	MON 6	TUE 7	WED 8	THU 9	FRI 10	SAT 11
LEO Jul 23 - Aug 22	1B 2A 3B	1B 2B 3B	1B 2A 3A	1AA 2AA 3AA	1X 2AA 3A	1B 2B 3A	1A 2B 3A

	SUN 5	MON 6	TUE 7	WED 8	THU 9	FRI 10	SAT 11
VIRGO Aug 23 - Sep 22	1A 2A 3A	1A 2A 3A	1B 2B 3B	1B 2BB 3BB	1BB 2B 3A	1A 2A 3B	1B 2B 3A

	SUN 5	MON 6	TUE 7	WED 8	THU 9	FRI 10	SAT 11
LIBRA Sep 23 - Oct 22	1B 2A 3A	1A 2A 3AA	1AA 2AA 3AA	1AA 2W 3A	1A 2B 3B	1B 2B 3A	1A 2A 3B

	SUN 5	MON 6	TUE 7	WED 8	THU 9	FRI 10	SAT 11
SCORPIO Oct 23 - Nov 22	1B 2B 3A	1A 2A 3A	1B 2B 3A	1B 2B 3B	1A 2A 3A	1A 2AA 3A	1B 2A 3B

	SUN 5	MON 6	TUE 7	WED 8	THU 9	FRI 10	SAT 11
SAGITTARIUS Nov 23 - Dec 21	1B 2B 3B	1A 2A 3B	1B 2B 3A	1A 2B 3A	1A 2A 3A	1BB 2BB 3B	1B 2B 3B

YOUR LUCKY STARS
August 12 - 18
1984

CAPRICORN Dec 22 - Jan 19	SUN 12	MON 13	TUE 14	WED 15	THU 16	FRI 17	SAT 18
	1 B	1 A	1 A	1 B	1 B	1 A	1 B
	2 B	2 A	2 B	2 A	2 A	2 A	2 B
	3 B	3 A	3 B	3 B	3 A	3 B	3 A

AQUARIUS Jan 20 - Feb 19	SUN 12	MON 13	TUE 14	WED 15	THU 16	FRI 17	SAT 18
	1 A	1 A	1 AA	1 A	1 AA	1 B	1 B
	2 B	2 A	2 AA	2 A	2 A	2 B	2 A
	3 A	3 A	3 W	3 A	3 B	3 B	3 A

PISCES Feb 20 - Mar 20	SUN 12	MON 13	TUE 14	WED 15	THU 16	FRI 17	SAT 18
	1 B	1 A	1 B	1 B	1 A	1 A	1 A
	2 B	2 A	2 B	2 B	2 B	2 A	2 B
	3 A	3 A	3 B	3 A	3 B	3 A	3 B

ARIES Mar 21 - Apr 19	SUN 12	MON 13	TUE 14	WED 15	THU 16	FRI 17	SAT 18
	1 B	1 A	1 B	1 A	1 A	1 AA	1 A
	2 A	2 B	2 B	2 A	2 A	2 A	2 A
	3 A	3 B	3 A	3 A	3 A	3 A	3 B

TAURUS Apr 20 - May 20	SUN 12	MON 13	TUE 14	WED 15	THU 16	FRI 17	SAT 18
	1 A	1 B	1 BB	1 BB	1 B	1 A	1 A
	2 B	2 BB	2 X	2 BB	2 A	2 A	2 B
	3 B	3 BB	3 BB	3 B	3 A	3 A	3 A

GEMINI May 21 - Jun 20	SUN 12	MON 13	TUE 14	WED 15	THU 16	FRI 17	SAT 18
	1 A	1 B	1 B	1 A	1 A	1 B	1 A
	2 A	2 B	2 A	2 A	2	2 B	2 A
	3 B	3 B	3 A	3 A	3 B	3 A	3 A

your lucky stars
August 12 - 18
1984

	SUN 12	MON 13	TUE 14	WED 15	THU 16	FRI 17	SAT 18
CANCER jun 21 - jul 22	1B 2B 3B	1B 2A 3A	1A 2A 3B	1BB 2BB 3B	1B 2A 3A	1A 2A 3A	1A 2A 3A
LEO jul 23 - aug 22	1A 2A 3B	1B 2A 3AA	1A 2A 3B	1B 2B 3A	1A 2A 3A	1A 2B 3B	1B 2A 3B
VIRGO aug 23 - sep 22	1B 2B 3A	1A 2B 3B	1B 2A 3A	1A 2B 3B	1A 2AA 3AA	1A 2A 3A	1A 2B 3A
LIBRA sep 23 - oct 22	1B 2A 3A	1A 2A 3B	1BB 2BB 3B	1A 2A 3A	1A 2A 3B	1B 2B 3B	1B 2B 3A
SCORPIO oct 23 - nov 22	1A 2A 3B	1B 2B 3A	1A 2A 3A	1AA 2AA 3A	1AA 2W 3AA	1A 2B 3B	1B 2A 3A
SAGITTARIUS nov 23 - dec 21	1B 2A 3B	1B 2B 3A	1A 2A 3B	1A 2A 3A	1B 2A 3A	1B 2B 3B	1A 2A 3B

your lucky stars
August 19 - 25
1984

CAPRICORN dec 22 - jan 19	SUN 19	MON 20	TUE 21	WED 22	THU 23	FRI 24	SAT 25
	1 A	1 B	1 B	1 A	1 BB	1 X	1 B
	2 B	2 B	2 A	2 B	2 BB	2 B	2 A
	3 B	3 B	3 A	3 B	3 X	3 B	3 A

AQUARIUS jan 20 - feb 19	SUN 19	MON 20	TUE 21	WED 22	THU 23	FRI 24	SAT 25
	1 A	1 A	1 B	1 A	1 A	1 A	1 B
	2 B	2 A	2 B	2 A	2 AA	2 B	2 A
	3 A	3 B	3 A	3 A	3 A	3 B	3 A

PISCES feb 20 - mar 20	SUN 19	MON 20	TUE 21	WED 22	THU 23	FRI 24	SAT 25
	1 B	1 A	1 B	1 B	1 A	1 A	1 A
	2 A	2 B	2 B	2 B	2 A	2 A	2 A
	3 A	3 B	3 B	3 B	3 A	3 A	3 A

ARIES mar 21 - apr 19	SUN 19	MON 20	TUE 21	WED 22	THU 23	FRI 24	SAT 25
	1 A	1 A	1 A	1 AA	1 A	1 B	1 B
	2 B	2 A	2 W	2 AA	2 A	2 B	2 B
	3 A	3 A	3 AA	3 AA	3 B	3 B	3 A

TAURUS apr 20 - may 20	SUN 19	MON 20	TUE 21	WED 22	THU 23	FRI 24	SAT 25
	1 A	1 B	1 B	1 A	1 A	1 B	1 B
	2 A	2 A	2 B	2 A	2 A	2 B	2 A
	3 B	3 A	3 B	3 A	3 A	3 B	3 A

GEMINI may 21 - jun 20	SUN 19	MON 20	TUE 21	WED 22	THU 23	FRI 24	SAT 25
	1 B	1 B	1 A	1 A	1 B	1 A	1 A
	2 A	2 B	2 A	2 A	2 B	2 A	2 A
	3 B	3 B	3 A	3 B	3 B	3 A	3 A

78

YOUR LUCKY STARS

August 19 - 25

1984

	SUN 19	MON 20	TUE 21	WED 22	THU 23	FRI 24	SAT 25
CANCER Jun 21 - Jul 22	1A 2B 3B	1B 2B 3A	1A 2A 3A	1A 2B 3B	1B 2B 3B	1B 2B 3A	1A 2B 3B
	SUN 19	MON 20	TUE 21	WED 22	THU 23	FRI 24	SAT 25
LEO Jul 23 - Aug 22	1B 2A 3A	1B 2B 3B	1B 2B 3B	1B 2B 3AA	1AA 2A 3A	1A 2A 3A	1A 2A 3A
	SUN 19	MON 20	TUE 21	WED 22	THU 23	FRI 24	SAT 25
VIRGO Aug 23 - Sep 22	1B 2B 3B	1B 2A 3A	1B 2B 3B	1B 2B 3A	1A 2A 3A	1A 2B 3A	1A 2B 3A
	SUN 19	MON 20	TUE 21	WED 22	THU 23	FRI 24	SAT 25
LIBRA Sep 23 - Oct 22	1A 2A 3B	1B 2B 3A	1A 2AA 3AA	1W 2AA 3AA	1A 2B 3B	1B 2B 3A	1A 2A 3A
	SUN 19	MON 20	TUE 21	WED 22	THU 23	FRI 24	SAT 25
SCORPIO Oct 23 - Nov 22	1A 2B 3A	1A 2B 3B	1B 2B 3A	1A 2A 3A	1B 2B 3A	1B 2B 3B	1A 2A 3A
	SUN 19	MON 20	TUE 21	WED 22	THU 23	FRI 24	SAT 25
SAGITTARIUS Nov 23 - Dec 21	1A 2A 3B	1B 2B 3B	1B 2B 3A	1A 2B 3A	1A 2B 3B	1B 2B 3B	1A 2B 3B

79

YOUR LUCKY STARS

August 26 – September 1
1984

CAPRICORN DEC 22 - JAN 19	SUN 26	MON 27	TUE 28	WED 29	THU 30	FRI 31	SAT 1
	1A	1B	1B	1A	1B	1B	1B
	2A	2B	2B	2A	2A	2B	2B
	3B	3B	3A	3B	3A	3B	3A

AQUARIUS JAN 20 - FEB 19	SUN 26	MON 27	TUE 28	WED 29	THU 30	FRI 31	SAT 1
	1A	1A	1B	1A	1AA	1A	1A
	2B	2B	2B	2A	2A	2A	2B
	3A	3B	3B	3AA	3A	3A	3A

PISCES FEB 20 - MAR 20	SUN 26	MON 27	TUE 28	WED 29	THU 30	FRI 31	SAT 1
	1B	1A	1B	1A	1A	1B	1A
	2B	2A	2B	2B	2A	2B	2A
	3A	3B	3B	3A	3B	3A	3B

ARIES MAR 21 - APR 19	SUN 26	MON 27	TUE 28	WED 29	THU 30	FRI 31	SAT 1
	1B	1B	1A	1W	1A	1B	1B
	2B	2B	2A	2W	2A	2B	2A
	3B	3A	3A	3AA	3A	3B	3A

TAURUS APR 20 - MAY 20	SUN 26	MON 27	TUE 28	WED 29	THU 30	FRI 31	SAT 1
	1B	1A	1B	1BB	1A	1A	1B
	2A	2A	2B	2BB	2A	2A	2B
	3B	3B	3BB	3BB	3A	3B	3B

GEMINI MAY 21 - JUN 20	SUN 26	MON 27	TUE 28	WED 29	THU 30	FRI 31	SAT 1
	1B	1A	1A	1B	1A	1B	1B
	2A	2A	2A	2A	2A	2A	2A
	3A	3A	3B	3A	3B	3B	3B

YOUR LUCKY STARS

August 26 - September 1
1984

	SUN 26	MON 27	TUE 28	WED 29	THU 30	FRI 31	SAT 1
CANCER jun 21 - jul 22	1 A 2 B 3 B	1 B 2 A 3 A	1 A 2 A 3 B	1 B 2 B 3 A	1 A 2 B 3 A	1 AA 2 AA 3 AA	1 A 2 B 3 B
LEO jul 23 - aug 22	1 A 2 A 3 A	1 B 2 A 3 A	1 A 2 A 3 A	1 A 2 A 3 B	1 B 2 B 3 B	1 B 2 B 3 B	1 B 2 B 3 B
VIRGO aug 23 - sep 22	1 A 2 B 3 B	1 A 2 A 3 A	1 B 2 B 3 B	1 B 2 A 3 A	1 A 2 A 3 A	1 B 2 B 3 B	1 A 2 A 3 B
LIBRA sep 23 - oct 22	1 B 2 A 3 A	1 A 2 B 3 B	1 B 2 A 3 A	1 A 2 B 3 B	1 A 2 B 3 A	1 A 2 B 3 B	1 B 2 A 3 B
SCORPIO oct 23 - nov 22	1 B 2 B 3 A	1 A 2 A 3 A	1 A 2 A 3 A	1 B 2 B 3 B	1 B 2 B 3 A	1 B 2 B 3 A	1 A 2 A 3 A
SAGITTARIUS nov 23 - dec 21	1 B 2 B 3 A	1 A 2 A 3 B	1 B 2 B 3 BB	1 X 2 X 3 BB	1 BB 2 BB 3 B	1 B 2 B 3 B	1 A 2 A 3 B

81

your lucky stars
September 2 - 8
1984

CAPRICORN dec 22 - jan 19	SUN 2	MON 3	TUE 4	WED 5	THU 6	FRI 7	SAT 8
	1A	1B	1B	1A	1B	1AA	1AA
	2A	2B	2A	2B	2A	2AA	2AA
	3B	3B	3A	3B	3A	3AA	3A

AQUARIUS jan 20 - feb 19	SUN 2	MON 3	TUE 4	WED 5	THU 6	FRI 7	SAT 8
	1A	1A	1A	1B	1B	1A	1A
	2B	2B	2A	2B	2A	2B	2A
	3A	3B	3A	3B	3A	3B	3A

PISCES feb 20 - mar 20	SUN 2	MON 3	TUE 4	WED 5	THU 6	FRI 7	SAT 8
	1B	1A	1B	1A	1A	1B	1B
	2B	2A	2B	2A	2A	2B	2B
	3A	3A	3A	3A	3B	3B	3B

ARIES mar 21 - apr 19	SUN 2	MON 3	TUE 4	WED 5	THU 6	FRI 7	SAT 8
	1A	1B	1A	1AA	1AA	1A	1A
	2B	2B	2AA	2W	2AA	2A	2A
	3B	3A	3AA	3AA	3AA	3A	3B

TAURUS apr 20 - may 20	SUN 2	MON 3	TUE 4	WED 5	THU 6	FRI 7	SAT 8
	1A	1A	1A	1A	1B	1A	1B
	2A	2A	2A	2B	2B	2A	2B
	3A	3A	3A	3B	3A	3A	3A

GEMINI may 21 - jun 20	SUN 2	MON 3	TUE 4	WED 5	THU 6	FRI 7	SAT 8
	1B	1B	1A	1A	1B	1BB	1X
	2A	2B	2A	2A	2BB	2BB	2A
	3B	3A	3A	3B	3BB	3BB	3B

YOUR LUCKY STARS
September 2 - 8
1984

	SUN 2	MON 3	TUE 4	WED 5	THU 6	FRI 7	SAT 8
CANCER Jun 21 - Jul 22	1B 2A 3A	1A 2A 3A	1A 2A 3B	1B 2B 3B	1B 2B 3B	1B 2A 3A	1A 2B 3A
LEO Jul 23 - Aug 22	1B 2B 3A	1A 2A 3A	1A 2A 3A	1A 2A 3B	1B 2B 3BB	1BB 2BB 3BB	1X 2BB 3B
VIRGO Aug 23 - Sep 22	1B 2A 3B	1B 2B 3B	1B 2B 3A	1A 2A 3B	1B 2B 3B	1B 2A 3A	1A 2A 3B
LIBRA Sep 23 - Oct 22	1A 2A 3B	1B 2B 3A	1BB 2BB 3BB	1B 2B 3A	1A 2A 3A	1A 2AA 3AA	1W 2AA 3AA
SCORPIO Oct 23 - Nov 22	1A 2B 3A	1B 2B 3B	1A 2B 3A	1A 2A 3B	1B 2B 3B	1B 2B 3B	1B 2B 3A
SAGITTARIUS Nov 23 - Dec 21	1 A 2 B 3 A	1 A 2 A 3 A	1 A 2 AA 3 AA	1 AA 2 A 3 A	1 A 2 A 3 B	1 B 2 B 3 A	1 A 2 B 3 B

your lucky stars
September 9 - 15
1984

CAPRICORN	SUN 9	MON 10	TUE 11	WED 12	THU 13	FRI 14	SAT 15
DEC 22 - JAN 19	1 A	1 B	1 B	1 A	1 A	1 AA	1 A
	2 A	2 B	2 B	2 A	2 AA	2 AA	2 A
	3 B	3 B	3 A	3 A	3 AA	3 A	3 B

AQUARIUS	SUN 9	MON 10	TUE 11	WED 12	THU 13	FRI 14	SAT 15
JAN 20 - FEB 19	1 B	1 A	1 B	1 A	1 A	1 A	1 B
	2 A	2 A	2 B	2 A	2 A	2 A	2 B
	3 B	3 B	3 B	3 A	3 A	3 B	3 B

PISCES	SUN 9	MON 10	TUE 11	WED 12	THU 13	FRI 14	SAT 15
FEB 20 - MAR 20	1 B	1 B	1 A	1 A	1 B	1 BB	1 B
	2 B	2 B	2 B	2 A	2 BB	2 X	2 B
	3 A	3 B	3 B	3 B	3 BB	3 B	3 AA

ARIES	SUN 9	MON 10	TUE 11	WED 12	THU 13	FRI 14	SAT 15
MAR 21 - APR 19	1 B	1 A	1 A	1 B	1 B	1 B	1 A
	2 A	2 A	2 A	2 B	2 B	2 B	2 B
	3 A	3 B	3 A	3 B	3 BB	3 A	3 B

TAURUS	SUN 9	MON 10	TUE 11	WED 12	THU 13	FRI 14	SAT 15
APR 20 - MAY 20	1 A	1 A	1 A	1 B	1 A	1 B	1 A
	2 B	2 A	2 A	2 A	2 A	2 B	2 A
	3 A	3 B	3 B	3 A	3 A	3 B	3 B

GEMINI	SUN 9	MON 10	TUE 11	WED 12	THU 13	FRI 14	SAT 15
MAY 21 - JUN 20	1 AA	1 AA	1 W	1 A	1 B	1 B	1 B
	2 AA	2 A	2 AA	2 A	2 B	2 B	2 A
	3 AA	3 W	3 AA	3 A	3 B	3 B	3 A

YOUR LUCKY STARS

September 9 - 15

1984

CANCER Jun 21 - Jul 22	SUN 9	MON 10	TUE 11	WED 12	THU 13	FRI 14	SAT 15
	1A	1B	1A	1B	1B	1A	1A
	2A	2B	2A	2BB	2A	2A	2A
	3B	3B	3B	3BB	3A	3A	3A

LEO Jul 23 - Aug 22	SUN 9	MON 10	TUE 11	WED 12	THU 13	FRI 14	SAT 15
	1B	1A	1B	1A	1AA	1W	1B
	2B	2A	2A	2A	2AA	2AA	2B
	3A	3A	3A	3A	3AA	3A	3B

VIRGO Aug 23 - Sep 22	SUN 9	MON 10	TUE 11	WED 12	THU 13	FRI 14	SAT 15
	1A	1A	1A	1B	1A	1A	1AA
	2B	2A	2B	2B	2A	2AA	2A
	3A	3A	3B	3B	3A	3AA	3A

LIBRA Sep 23 - Oct 22	SUN 9	MON 10	TUE 11	WED 12	THU 13	FRI 14	SAT 15
	1B	1B	1A	1B	1B	1X	1B
	2A	2B	2B	2A	2BB	2BB	2B
	3B	3A	3B	3A	3BB	3BB	3B

SCORPIO Oct 23 - Nov 22	SUN 9	MON 10	TUE 11	WED 12	THU 13	FRI 14	SAT 15
	1A	1B	1B	1B	1A	1A	1A
	2A	2A	2B	2A	2AA	2A	2B
	3B	3A	3B	3A	3AA	3A	3B

SAGITTARIUS Nov 23 - Dec 21	SUN 9	MON 10	TUE 11	WED 12	THU 13	FRI 14	SAT 15
	1B	1B	1A	1A	1A	1B	1B
	2B	2B	2A	2AA	2A	2B	2B
	3B	3A	3A	3AA	3B	3B	3A

your lucky stars
September 16 - 22
1984

CAPRICORN	SUN 16	MON 17	TUE 18	WED 19	THU 20	FRI 21	SAT 22
δεc 22 - jan 19	1 A	1 B	1 B	1 A	1 B	1 B	1 A
	2 A	2 A	2 B	2 A	2 B	2 B	2 A
	3 B	3 A	3 A	3 D	3 B	3 B	3 A

AQUARIUS	SUN 16	MON 17	TUE 18	WED 19	THU 20	FRI 21	SAT 22
jan 20 - feb 19	1 A	1 A	1 B	1 AA	1 A	1 A	1 B
	2 B	2 B	2 A	2 AA	2 A	2 B	2 B
	3 A	3 B	3 A	3 W	3 A	3 B	3 B

PISCES	SUN 16	MON 17	TUE 18	WED 19	THU 20	FRI 21	SAT 22
feb 20 - mar 20	1 A	1 A	1 A	1 A	1 A	1 B	1 A
	2 A	2 A	2 A	2 A	2 B	2 B	2 B
	3 A	3 A	3 A	3 A	3 B	3 A	3 B

ARIES	SUN 16	MON 17	TUE 18	WED 19	THU 20	FRI 21	SAT 22
mar 21 - apr 19	1 B	1 A	1 B	1 A	1 A	1 AA	1 A
	2 B	2 B	2 A	2 A	2 A	2 AA	2 A
	3 A	3 B	3 A	3 A	3 AA	3 A	3 B

TAURUS	SUN 16	MON 17	TUE 18	WED 19	THU 20	FRI 21	SAT 22
apr 20 - may 20	1 A	1 B	1 A	1 A	1 A	1 BB	1 BB
	2 B	2 B	2 A	2 A	2 A	2 BB	2 BB
	3 B	3 A	3 A	3 A	3 B	3 X	3 BB

GEMINI	SUN 16	MON 17	TUE 18	WED 19	THU 20	FRI 21	SAT 22
may 21 - jun 20	1 B	1 B	1 B	1 A	1 B	1 A	1 A
	2 A	2 B	2 A	2 A	2 B	2 A	2 B
	3 B	3 B	3 A	3 A	3 B	3 A	3 B

YOUR LUCKY STARS
September 16 - 22
1984

CANCER Jun 21 - Jul 22	SUN 16	MON 17	TUE 18	WED 19	THU 20	FRI 21	SAT 22
	1A	1B	1A	1A	1B	1BB	1B
	2B	2B	2A	2A	2BB	2B	2B
	3B	3B	3A	3A	3BB	3B	3A

LEO Jul 23 - Aug 22	SUN 16	MON 17	TUE 18	WED 19	THU 20	FRI 21	SAT 22
	1A	1A	1A	1B	1A	1B	1B
	2B	2A	2A	2B	2A	2B	2A
	3A	3A	3A	3A	3A	3A	3B

VIRGO Aug 23 - Sep 22	SUN 16	MON 17	TUE 18	WED 19	THU 20	FRI 21	SAT 22
	1A	1B	1A	1AA	1AA	1A	1B
	2A	2B	2A	2W	2AA	2A	2B
	3B	3A	3AA	3AA	3AA	3B	3B

LIBRA Sep 23 - Oct 22	SUN 16	MON 17	TUE 18	WED 19	THU 20	FRI 21	SAT 22
	1A	1A	1B	1BB	1A	1A	1A
	2A	2A	2B	2B	2A	2AA	2A
	3A	3B	3BB	3A	3A	3AA	3B

SCORPIO Oct 23 - Nov 22	SUN 16	MON 17	TUE 18	WED 19	THU 20	FRI 21	SAT 22
	1B	1B	1B	1A	1A	1B	1A
	2A	2B	2B	2A	2A	2B	2B
	3B	3B	3A	3A	3B	3A	3A

SAGITTARIUS Nov 23 - Dec 21	SUN 16	MON 17	TUE 18	WED 19	THU 20	FRI 21	SAT 22
	1B	1B	1A	1A	1A	1A	1A
	2B	2B	2A	2A	2A	2A	2B
	3A	3B	3A	3B	3A	3A	3B

your lucky stars

September 23 - 29
1984

CAPRICORN DEC 22 - JAN 19	SUN 23	MON 24	TUE 25	WED 26	THU 27	FRI 28	SAT 29
	1B	1B	1B	1A	1A	1BB	1B
	2B	2B	2A	2A	2B	2BB	2B
	3B	3B	3A	3A	3B	3B	3A

AQUARIUS JAN 20 - FEB 19	SUN 23	MON 24	TUE 25	WED 26	THU 27	FRI 28	SAT 29
	1A	1A	1B	1A	1AA	1A	1B
	2B	2A	2B	2A	2AA	2A	2A
	3A	3B	3B	3A	3A	3AA	3B

PISCES FEB 20 - MAR 20	SUN 23	MON 24	TUE 25	WED 26	THU 27	FRI 28	SAT 29
	1A	1B	1A	1BB	1X	1B	1A
	2A	2A	2A	2BB	2BB	2B	2A
	3B	3A	3B	3BB	3BB	3A	3B

ARIES MAR 21 - APR 19	SUN 23	MON 24	TUE 25	WED 26	THU 27	FRI 28	SAT 29
	1B	1B	1A	1B	1A	1A	1B
	2A	2A	2A	2B	2A	2A	2A
	3B	3A	3B	3A	3A	3B	3A

TAURUS APR 20 - MAY 20	SUN 23	MON 24	TUE 25	WED 26	THU 27	FRI 28	SAT 29
	1B	1B	1A	1AA	1AA	1A	1A
	2B	2B	2AA	2W	2AA	2B	2B
	3A	3B	3AA	3A	3AA	3B	3A

GEMINI MAY 21 - JUN 20	SUN 23	MON 24	TUE 25	WED 26	THU 27	FRI 28	SAT 29
	1B	1A	1B	1BB	1B	1B	1A
	2A	2A	2B	2BB	2B	2A	2A
	3A	3B	3BB	3B	3B	3A	3A

your lucky stars

September 23 - 29
1984

CANCER Jun 21 - Jul 22	SUN 23	MON 24	TUE 25	WED 26	THU 27	FRI 28	SAT 29
	1B	1B	1B	1A	1AA	1A	1B
	2A	2B	2A	2A	2AA	2A	2B
	3B	3B	3A	3AA	3A	3A	3A

LEO Jul 23 - Aug 22	SUN 23	MON 24	TUE 25	WED 26	THU 27	FRI 28	SAT 29
	1A	1AA	1A	1A	1B	1B	1A
	2A	2AA	2B	2B	2B	2A	2A
	3A	3A	3A	3A	3B	3A	3B

VIRGO Aug 23 - Sep 22	SUN 23	MON 24	TUE 25	WED 26	THU 27	FRI 28	SAT 29
	1A	1A	1B	1A	1B	1B	1B
	2B	2B	2A	2A	2A	2B	2B
	3B	3B	3A	3B	3A	3B	3B

LIBRA Sep 23 - Oct 22	SUN 23	MON 24	TUE 25	WED 26	THU 27	FRI 28	SAT 29
	1A	1B	1A	1A	1A	1B	1A
	2B	2B	2A	2B	2A	2A	2B
	3B	3A	3A	3B	3B	3A	3A

SCORPIO Oct 23 - Nov 22	SUN 23	MON 24	TUE 25	WED 26	THU 27	FRI 28	SAT 29
	1A	1B	1A	1A	1A	1B	1B
	2A	2A	2A	2A	2A	2B	2A
	3B	3B	3A	3A	3B	3B	3B

SAGITTARIUS Nov 23 - Dec 21	SUN 23	MON 24	TUE 25	WED 26	THU 27	FRI 28	SAT 29
	1A	1B	1B	1B	1A	1A	1B
	2A	2B	2B	2B	2A	2A	2B
	3B	3A	3B	3A	3A	3B	3A

YOUR LUCKY STARS

September 30 - October 6
1984

	SUN 30	MON 1	TUE 2	WED 3	THU 4	FRI 5	SAT 6
CAPRICORN dec 22 - jan 19	1A 2B 3A	1 A 2 A 3 A	1B 2B 3B	1BB 2BB 3BB	1B 2B 3A	1A 2A 3A	1A 2A 3B
AQUARIUS jan 20 - feb 19	1A 2A 3A	1 A 2 A 3 B	1B 2A 3A	1AA 2AA 3AA	1AA 2AA 3W	1AA 2A 3B	1B 2B 3B
PISCES feb 20 - mar 20	1B 2B 3A	1 A 2 B 3 B	1B 2BB 3BB	1A 2B 3B	1B 2B 3A	1A 2B 3B	1B 2A 3B
ARIES mar 21 - apr 19	1A 2A 3B	1 A 2 A 3 B	1B 2B 3A	1A 2B 3B	1B 2A 3A	1A 2A 3B	1B 2B 3A
TAURUS apr 20 - may 20	1B 2A 3A	1 A 2 A 3 A	1A 2B 3B	1A 2AA 3AA	1B 2B 3B	1B 2A 3A	1A 2B 3A
GEMINI may 21 - jun 20	1B 2A 3B	1 B 2 B 3 B	1A 2A 3A	1A 2B 3B	1B 2A 3A	1A 2A 3AA	1AA 2A 3A

your lucky stars

September 30 - October 6

1984

CANCER Jun 21 - Jul 22	SUN 30	MON 1	TUE 2	WED 3	THU 4	FRI 5	SAT 6
	1 A	1 B	1 AA	1 A	1 A	1 B	1 B
	2 B	2 A	2 AA	2 B	2 A	2 B	2 B
	3 B	3 AA	3 W	3 A	3 A	3 B	3 A

LEO Jul 23 - Aug 22	SUN 30	MON 1	TUE 2	WED 3	THU 4	FRI 5	SAT 6
	1 A	1 A	1 A	1 A	1 B	1 B	1 B
	2 B	2 A	2 A	2 A	2 B	2 A	2 B
	3 A	3 A	3 A	3 A	3 B	3 B	3 A

VIRGO Aug 23 - Sep 22	SUN 30	MON 1	TUE 2	WED 3	THU 4	FRI 5	SAT 6
	1 B	1 A	1 A	1 B	1 A	1 A	1 A
	2 B	2 A	2 A	2 B	2 B	2 A	2 A
	3 A	3 B	3 A	3 B	3 B	3 A	3 A

LIBRA Sep 23 - Oct 22	SUN 30	MON 1	TUE 2	WED 3	THU 4	FRI 5	SAT 6
	1 B	1 B	1 B	1 A	1 B	1 AA	1 A
	2 A	2 A	2 A	2 A	2 A	2 AA	2 B
	3 B	3 B	3 A	3 B	3 A	3 A	3 A

SCORPIO Oct 23 - Nov 22	SUN 30	MON 1	TUE 2	WED 3	THU 4	FRI 5	SAT 6
	1 B	1 B	1 BB	1 B	1 A	1 A	1 A
	2 B	2 B	2 BB	2 B	2 A	2 B	2 B
	3 B	3 B	3 X	3 B	3 B	3 B	3 B

SAGITTARIUS Nov 23 - Dec 21	SUN 30	MON 1	TUE 2	WED 3	THU 4	FRI 5	SAT 6
	1 A	1 A	1 B	1 B	1 A	1 A	1 A
	2 B	2 A	2 A	2 B	2 A	2 B	2 B
	3 B	3 B	3 A	3 A	3 A	3 A	3 B

your lucky stars
October 7 - 13
1984

CAPRICORN dec 22 - jan 19	SUN 7	MON 8	TUE 9	WED 10	THU 11	FRI 12	SAT 13
	1 A	1 B	1B	1A	1B	1A	1B
	2 B	2 B	2A	2A	2B	2A	2B
	3 B	3 B	3A	3B	3B	3A	3B

AQUARIUS jan 20 - feb 19	SUN 7	MON 8	TUE 9	WED 10	THU 11	FRI 12	SAT 13
	1 B	1 B	1A	1B	1B	1A	1B
	2 A	2 A	2AA	2B	2B	2B	2A
	3 B	3 A	3A	3B	3A	3B	3A

PISCES feb 20 - mar 20	SUN 7	MON 8	TUE 9	WED 10	THU 11	FRI 12	SAT 13
	1 A	1 B	1A	1B	1BB	1B	1A
	2 A	2 A	2A	2B	2BB	2B	2A
	3 B	3 A	3A	3BB	3BB	3A	3A

ARIES mar 21 - apr 19	SUN 7	MON 8	TUE 9	WED 10	THU 11	FRI 12	SAT 13
	1 A	1 A	1A	1A	1A	1A	1A
	2 B	2 B	2A	2B	2B	2B	2A
	3 A	3 B	3A	3A	3B	3A	3AA

TAURUS apr 20 - may 20	SUN 7	MON 8	TUE 9	WED 10	THU 11	FRI 12	SAT 13
	1 A	1 A	1A	1AA	1B	1A	1AA
	2 A	2 A	2A	2A	2B	2A	2W
	3 A	3 B	3AA	3B	3A	3AA	3AA

GEMINI may 21 - jun 20	SUN 7	MON 8	TUE 9	WED 10	THU 11	FRI 12	SAT 13
	1 B	1 A	1A	1B	1A	1A	1B
	2 B	2 A	2A	2B	2A	2B	2B
	3 A	3 A	3B	3A	3A	3BB	3A

YOUR LUCKY STARS
October 7 - 13
1984

CANCER Jun 21 - Jul 22	SUN 7	MON 8	TUE 9	WED 10	THU 11	FRI 12	SAT 13
	1 B	1 B	1 A	1 A	1 B	1 B	1 B
	2 B	2 A	2 A	2 A	2 A	2 B	2 A
	3 B	3 A	3 A	3 B	3 A	3 B	3 A

LEO Jul 23 - Aug 22	SUN 7	MON 8	TUE 9	WED 10	THU 11	FRI 12	SAT 13
	1 B	1 B	1 A	1 AA	1 A	1 A	1 A
	2 B	2 B	2 A	2 AA	2 B	2 A	2 B
	3 A	3 A	3 A	3 AA	3 B	3 A	3 A

VIRGO Aug 23 - Sep 22	SUN 7	MON 8	TUE 9	WED 10	THU 11	FRI 12	SAT 13
	1 B	1 A	1 B	1 B	1 A	1 A	1 A
	2 A	2 B	2 BB	2 B	2 B	2 A	2 A
	3 A	3 A	3 BB	3 A	3 B	3 A	3 B

LIBRA Sep 23 - Oct 22	SUN 7	MON 8	TUE 9	WED 10	THU 11	FRI 12	SAT 13
	1 B	1 A	1 A	1 B	1 B	1 A	1 A
	2 A	2 BB	2 A	2 B	2 B	2 AA	2 A
	3 A	3 A	3 B	3 B	3 A	3 AA	3 A

SCORPIO Oct 23 - Nov 22	SUN 7	MON 8	TUE 9	WED 10	THU 11	FRI 12	SAT 13
	1 B	1 BB	1 B	1 A	1 B	1 A	1 A
	2 BB	2 BB	2 A	2 A	2 B	2 A	2 AA
	3 X	3 BB	3 A	3 B	3 B	3 A	3 A

SAGITTARIUS Nov 23 - Dec 21	SUN 7	MON 8	TUE 9	WED 10	THU 11	FRI 12	SAT 13
	1 A	1 A	1 B	1 A	1 B	1 B	1 B
	2 A	2 A	2 B	2 B	2 B	2 BB	2 A
	3 A	3 B	3 A	3 B	3 B	3 BB	3 A

YOUR LUCKY STARS

October 14 - 20
1984

CAPRICORN ᴅᴇᴄ 22 - ᴊᴀɴ 19	SUN 14	MON 15	TUE 16	WED 17	THU 18	FRI 19	SAT 20
	1AA	1 A	1A	1B	1B	1A	1B
	2A	2 B	2A	2BB	2B	2A	2B
	3A	3 B	3A	3BB	3A	3B	3B

AQUARIUS ᴊᴀɴ 20 - ꜰᴇʙ 19	SUN 14	MON 15	TUE 16	WED 17	THU 18	FRI 19	SAT 20
	1B	1 A	1A	1B	1A	1B	1A
	2B	2 A	2A	2B	2A	2B	2A
	3A	3 A	3A	3B	3A	3B	3B

PISCES ꜰᴇʙ 20 - ᴍᴀʀ 20	SUN 14	MON 15	TUE 16	WED 17	THU 18	FRI 19	SAT 20
	1A	1 B	1A	1B	1B	1B	1B
	2B	2 B	2A	2B	2B	2B	2B
	3B	3 A	3A	3B	3B	3B	3A

ARIES ᴍᴀʀ 21 - ᴀᴘʀ 19	SUN 14	MON 15	TUE 16	WED 17	THU 18	FRI 19	SAT 20
	1A	1 B	1BB	1B	1BB	1B	1A
	2A	2 B	2X	2B	2B	2B	2B
	3B	3 B	3BB	3B	3B	3A	3B

TAURUS ᴀᴘʀ 20 - ᴍᴀʏ 20	SUN 14	MON 15	TUE 16	WED 17	THU 18	FRI 19	SAT 20
	1A	1 A	1A	1BB	1A	1A	1B
	2B	2 A	2B	2B	2A	2A	2A
	3B	3 A	3B	3B	3A	3B	3A

GEMINI ᴍᴀʏ 21 - ᴊᴜɴ 20	SUN 14	MON 15	TUE 16	WED 17	THU 18	FRI 19	SAT 20
	1B	1 A	1A	1B	1A	1AA	1A
	2A	2 B	2A	2B	2W	2AA	2A
	3A	3 B	3B	3A	3AA	3AA	3A

YOUR LUCKY STARS

October 14 - 20

1984

	SUN 14	MON 15	TUE 16	WED 17	THU 18	FRI 19	SAT 20
CANCER Jun 21 - Jul 22	1A 2A 3B	1A 2A 3A	1A 2B 3A	1B 2B 3B	1B 2B 3A	1AA 2A 3A	1A 2A 3A
LEO Jul 23 - Aug 22	1B 2B 3A	1A 2A 3A	1A 2B 3B	1B 2B 3B	1A 2A 3A	1A 2A 3A	1A 2A 3A
VIRGO Aug 23 - Sep 22	1B 2A 3A	1A 2A 3B	1B 2B 3A	1A 2A 3A	1AA 2AA 3W	1W 2AA 3A	1B 2B 3B
LIBRA Sep 23 - Oct 22	1A 2B 3B	1B 2B 3B	1 B 2 B 3B	1BB 2BB 3B	1B 2B 3B	1A 2A 3A	1B 2B 3A
SCORPIO Oct 23 - Nov 22	1B 2A 3B	1A 2A 3B	1B 2B 3B	1B 2B 3B	1A 2A 3A	1A 2A 3A	1AA 2AA 3A
SAGITTARIUS Nov 23 - Dec 21	1A 2B 3A	1A 2A 3B	1B 2B 3B	1BB 2BB 3BB	1BB 2BB 3B	1B 2B 3B	1B 2B 3A

your lucky stars

October 21 - 27

1984

CAPRICORN Dec 22 - Jan 19	SUN 21	MON 22	TUE 23	WED 24	THU 25	FRI 26	SAT 27
	1B	1 A	1B	1A	1A	1A	1A
	2B	2 B	2B	2B	2AA	2A	2A
	3A	3 B	3A	3A	3A	3A	3A

AQUARIUS Jan 20 - Feb 19	SUN 21	MON 22	TUE 23	WED 24	THU 25	FRI 26	SAT 27
	1A	1 B	1B	1A	1B	1A	1B
	2A	2 B	2A	2A	2B	2A	2A
	3B	3 B	3A	3B	3B	3B	3A

PISCES Feb 20 - Mar 20	SUN 21	MON 22	TUE 23	WED 24	THU 25	FRI 26	SAT 27
	1A	1 B	1B	1A	1B	1X	1A
	2B	2 A	2A	2B	2B	2BB	2B
	3B	3 B	3A	3B	3A	3B	3B

ARIES Mar 21 - Apr 19	SUN 21	MON 22	TUE 23	WED 24	THU 25	FRI 26	SAT 27
	1A	1 A	1A	1B	1B	1B	1B
	2A	2 A	2B	2B	2B	2A	2A
	3A	3 A	3B	3B	3B	3B	3B

TAURUS Apr 20 - May 20	SUN 21	MON 22	TUE 23	WED 24	THU 25	FRI 26	SAT 27
	1B	1 AA	1A	1B	1A	1A	1A
	2B	2 A	2B	2B	2A	2A	2A
	3A	3 A	3B	3A	3B	3A	3B

GEMINI May 21 - Jun 20	SUN 21	MON 22	TUE 23	WED 24	THU 25	FRI 26	SAT 27
	1B	1 A	1A	1B	1A	1BB	1B
	2B	2 A	2B	2A	2B	2B	2B
	3A	3 A	3B	3A	3BB	3B	3A

your lucky stars

October 21 - 27
1984

CANCER Jun 21 - Jul 22	SUN 21	MON 22	TUE 23	WED 24	THU 25	FRI 26	SAT 27
	1A	1A	1AA	1AA	1B	1B	1A
	2A	2A	2AA	2A	2B	2B	2A
	3A	3AA	3W	3A	3B	3A	3A

LEO Jul 23 - Aug 22	SUN 21	MON 22	TUE 23	WED 24	THU 25	FRI 26	SAT 27
	1A	1B	1B	1A	1B	1A	1A
	2B	2B	2A	2B	2B	2A	2B
	3B	3B	3A	3B	3B	3A	3B

VIRGO Aug 23 - Sep 22	SUN 21	MON 22	TUE 23	WED 24	THU 25	FRI 26	SAT 27
	1B	1A	1A	1A	1B	1A	1B
	2A	2A	2A	2B	2B	2A	2B
	3A	3A	3A	3B	3A	3B	3A

LIBRA Sep 23 - Oct 22	SUN 21	MON 22	TUE 23	WED 24	THU 25	FRI 26	SAT 27
	1B	1A	1B	1A	1B	1BB	1B
	2B	2B	2B	2A	2BB	2X	2B
	3A	3B	3A	3B	3BB	3B	3B

SCORPIO Oct 23 - Nov 22	SUN 21	MON 22	TUE 23	WED 24	THU 25	FRI 26	SAT 27
	1A	1A	1B	1B	1A	1A	1B
	2A	2A	2BB	2A	2B	2A	2B
	3B	3A	3B	3A	3B	3A	3B

SAGITTARIUS Nov 23 - Dec 21	SUN 21	MON 22	TUE 23	WED 24	THU 25	FRI 26	SAT 27
	1A	1A	1B	1B	1A	1AA	1A
	2A	2B	2B	2B	2A	2AA	2B
	3A	3B	3B	3A	3W	3A	3B

YOUR LUCKY STARS
October 28 - November 3
1984

CAPRICORN Dec 22 - Jan 19	SUN 28	MON 29	TUE 30	WED 31	THU 1	FRI 2	SAT 3
	1 A	1 B	1 B	1 A	1 A	1 B	1 A
	2 A	2 B	2 B	2 A	2 A	2 A	2 A
	3 B	3 B	3 A	3 A	3 B	3 A	3 AA

AQUARIUS Jan 20 - Feb 19	SUN 28	MON 29	TUE 30	WED 31	THU 1	FRI 2	SAT 3
	1 A	1 B	1 A	1 A	1 B	1 B	1 A
	2 B	2 A	2 B	2 B	2 BB	2 A	2 A
	3 B	3 A	3 A	3 B	3 BB	3 A	3 A

PISCES Feb 20 - Mar 20	SUN 28	MON 29	TUE 30	WED 31	THU 1	FRI 2	SAT 3
	1 A	1 B	1 A	1 A	1 B	1 A	1 B
	2 B	2 B	2 A	2 A	2 B	2 A	2 A
	3 B	3 A	3 A	3 B	3 B	3 B	3 B

ARIES Mar 21 - Apr 19	SUN 28	MON 29	TUE 30	WED 31	THU 1	FRI 2	SAT 3
	1 B	1 A	1 B	1 BB	1 A	1 B	1 B
	2 B	2 A	2 B	2 B	2 A	2 B	2 B
	3 A	3 A	3 B	3 B	3 A	3 B	3 A

TAURUS Apr 20 - May 20	SUN 28	MON 29	TUE 30	WED 31	THU 1	FRI 2	SAT 3
	1 B	1 B	1 A	1 A	1 A	1 A	1 B
	2 B	2 A	2 A	2 A	2 A	2 B	2 B
	3 B	3 A	3 AA	3 A	3 A	3 B	3 B

GEMINI May 21 - Jun 20	SUN 28	MON 29	TUE 30	WED 31	THU 1	FRI 2	SAT 3
	1 A	1 A	1 A	1 A	1 B	1 B	1 A
	2 A	2 A	2 A	2 B	2 BB	2 A	2 B
	3 A	3 A	3 A	3 B	3 B	3 A	3 B

your lucky stars
October 28 - November 3
1984

	SUN 28	MON 29	TUE 30	WED 31	THU 1	FRI 2	SAT 3
CANCER Jun 21 - Jul 22	1A 2B 3B	1B 2A 3A	1A 2B 3A	1A 2A 3A	1A 2A 3B	1B 2B 3B	1B 2A 3A
LEO Jul 23 - Aug 22	1B 2A 3A	1A 2AA 3A	1A 2B 3B	1A 2A 3A	1AA 2W 3AA	1A 2A 3B	1B 2B 3B
VIRGO Aug 23 - Sep 22	1BB 2B 3B	1B 2B 3B	1B 2A 3AA	1AA 2AA 3A	1A 2A 3A	1A 2B 3B	1A 2A 3B
LIBRA Sep 23 - Oct 22	1A 2B 3A	1B 2B 3A	1A 2A 3B	1B 2A 3A	1A 2B 3B	1B 2B 3A	1A 2A 3A
SCORPIO Oct 23 - Nov 22	1B 2B 3B	1BB 2X 3BB	1BB 2B 3A	1A 2A 3A	1AA 2A 3A	1A 2A 3A	1A 2B 3B
SAGITTARIUS Nov 23 - Dec 21	1A 2B 3B	1A 2A 3A	1A 2A 3A	1A 2A 3A	1B 2B 3B	1A 2A 3B	1B 2A 3B

99

your lucky stars

November 4 - 10

1984

CAPRICORN
δec 22 - Jan 19

	SUN 4	MON 5	TUE 6	WED 7	THU 8	FRI 9	SAT 10
	1 B	1 A	1 B	1 B	1 B	1 AA	1 A
	2 B	2 B	2 B	2 BB	2 A	2 A	2 A
	3 A	3 B	3 B	3 B	3 A	3 A	3 A

AQUARIUS
Jan 20 - feb 19

	SUN 4	MON 5	TUE 6	WED 7	THU 8	FRI 9	SAT 10
	1 A	1 B	1 A	1 A	1 A	1 B	1 B
	2 A	2 A	2 B	2 A	2 AA	2 B	2 B
	3 B	3 A	3 A	3 A	3 A	3 B	3 BB

PISCES
feb 20 - mar 20

	SUN 4	MON 5	TUE 6	WED 7	THU 8	FRI 9	SAT 10
	1 B	1 A	1 A	1 B	1 B	1 B	1 A
	2 B	2 A	2 B	2 BB	2 B	2 B	2 B
	3 A	3 A	3 B	3 B	3 B	3 A	3 B

ARIES
mar 21 - apr 19

	SUN 4	MON 5	TUE 6	WED 7	THU 8	FRI 9	SAT 10
	1 A	1 B	1 B	1 A	1 B	1 A	1 AA
	2 B	2 B	2 B	2 B	2 B	2 A	2 A
	3 B	3 B	3 A	3 A	3 A	3 A	3 A

TAURUS
apr 20 - may 20

	SUN 4	MON 5	TUE 6	WED 7	THU 8	FRI 9	SAT 10
	1 A	1 A	1 B	1 A	1 AA	1 A	1 B
	2 B	2 A	2 B	2 A	2 W	2 A	2 A
	3 A	3 A	3 A	3 A	3 AA	3 B	3 A

GEMINI
may 21 - jun 20

	SUN 4	MON 5	TUE 6	WED 7	THU 8	FRI 9	SAT 10
	1 B	1 B	1 B	1 A	1 AA	1 B	1 A
	2 B	2 A	2 B	2 A	2 AA	2 B	2 A
	3 B	3 A	3 A	3 A	3 A	3 B	3 B

100

your lucky stars

November 4 - 10

1984

CANCER Jun 21 - Jul 22	SUN 4	MON 5	TUE 6	WED 7	THU 8	FRI 9	SAT 10
	1 A	1 A	1 A	1 B	1 A	1 A	1 A
	2 B	2 A	2 B	2 B	2 A	2 AA	2 B
	3 A	3 B	3 B	3 A	3 A	3 AA	3 B

LEO Jul 23 - Aug 22	SUN 4	MON 5	TUE 6	WED 7	THU 8	FRI 9	SAT 10
	1 A	1 B	1 A	1 A	1 B	1 B	1 B
	2 B	2 B	2 A	2 A	2 B	2 B	2 A
	3 B	3 A	3 A	3 B	3 A	3 B	3 B

VIRGO Aug 23 - Sep 22	SUN 4	MON 5	TUE 6	WED 7	THU 8	FRI 9	SAT 10
	1 A	1 A	1 B	1 A	1 AA	1 A	1 A
	2 B	2 B	2 A	2 A	2 A	2 A	2 B
	3 A	3 B	3 A	3 AA	3 A	3 A	3 B

LIBRA Sep 23 - Oct 22	SUN 4	MON 5	TUE 6	WED 7	THU 8	FRI 9	SAT 10
	1 B	1 B	1 A	1 A	1 AA	1 A	1 A
	2 A	2 B	2 A	2 A	2 W	2 A	2 B
	3 B	3 B	3 A	3 A	3 AA	3 A	3 A

SCORPIO Oct 23 - Nov 22	SUN 4	MON 5	TUE 6	WED 7	THU 8	FRI 9	SAT 10
	1 B	1 B	1 A	1 B	1 B	1 B	1 A
	2 B	2 B	2 A	2 A	2 B	2 B	2 A
	3 A	3 A	3 A	3 A	3 B	3 B	3 B

SAGITTARIUS Nov 23 - Dec 21	SUN 4	MON 5	TUE 6	WED 7	THU 8	FRI 9	SAT 10
	1 A	1 B	1 BB	1 BB	1 B	1 A	1 B
	2 A	2 B	2 X	2 BB	2 B	2 A	2 B
	3 A	3 BB	3 X	3 BB	3 B	3 B	3 A

101

your lucky stars
November 11 - 17
1984

CAPRICORN DEC 22 - JAN 19	SUN 11	MON 12	TUE 13	WED 14	THU 15	FRI 16	SAT 17
	1B	1A	1A	1A	1 AA	1AA	1B
	2B	2A	2A	2A	2 AA	2AA	2B
	3A	3A	3A	3A	3 AA	3A	3B

AQUARIUS JAN 20 - FEB 19	SUN 11	MON 12	TUE 13	WED 14	THU 15	FRI 16	SAT 17
	1A	1A	1B	1A	1A	1BB	1B
	2B	2B	2B	2A	2B	2BB	2B
	3A	3B	3A	3A	3B	3B	3A

PISCES FEB 20 - MAR 20	SUN 11	MON 12	TUE 13	WED 14	THU 15	FRI 16	SAT 17
	1A	1A	1A	1A	1W	1A	1B
	2A	2B	2A	2AA	2W	2A	2A
	3A	3B	3A	3AA	3AA	3A	3A

ARIES MAR 21 - APR 19	SUN 11	MON 12	TUE 13	WED 14	THU 15	FRI 16	SAT 17
	1B	1A	1B	1A	1A	1A	1A
	2A	2B	2B	2B	2A	2A	2B
	3A	3B	3A	3B	3A	3A	3A

TAURUS APR 20 - MAY 20	SUN 11	MON 12	TUE 13	WED 14	THU 15	FRI 16	SAT 17
	1A	1B	1B	1A	1AA	1AA	1A
	2B	2B	2B	2A	2AA	2AA	2A
	3B	3B	3A	3AA	3AA	3A	3A

GEMINI MAY 21 - JUN 20	SUN 11	MON 12	TUE 13	WED 14	THU 15	FRI 16	SAT 17
	1B	1B	1BB	1A	1B	1B	1B
	2B	2A	2BB	2A	2B	2B	2A
	3B	3A	3B	3A	3B	3B	3A

your lucky stars
November 11 - 17
1984

	SUN 11	MON 12	TUE 13	WED 14	THU 15	FRI 16	SAT 17
CANCER Jun 21 - Jul 22	1 B 2 B 3 A	1 A 2 A 3 A	1 A 2 A 3 B	1 B 2 B 3 B	1 A 2 A 3 B	1 B 2 B 3 A	1 A 2 B 3 B
LEO Jul 23 - Aug 22	1 A 2 A 3 A	1 A 2 A 3 A	1 A 2 B 3 B	1 B 2 B 3 B	1 X 2 X 3 X	1 BB 2 BB 3 B	1 B 2 A 3 B
VIRGO Aug 23 - Sep 22	1 A 2 B 3 B	1 B 2 B 3 A	1 A 2 B 3 B	1 A 2 A 3 A	1 A 2 B 3 B	1 A 2 B 3 B	1 B 2 B 3 A
LIBRA Sep 23 - Oct 22	1 A 2 B 3 A	1 B 2 A 3 B	1 B 2 B 3 A	1 A 2 A 3 A	1 A 2 AA 3 AA	1 A 2 A 3 B	1 B 2 A 3 A
SCORPIO Oct 23 - Nov 22	1 A 2 B 3 B	1 B 2 A 3 A	1 AA 2 AA 3 A	1 A 2 B 3 B	1 BB 2 BB 3 B	1 B 2 B 3 A	1 A 2 B 3 A
SAGITTARIUS Nov 23 - Dec 21	1 B 2 A 3 B	1 B 2 B 3 B	1 A 2 A 3 A	1 A 2 B 3 B	1 A 2 A 3 B	1 B 2 B 3 B	1 B 2 B 3 B

103

YOUR LUCKY STARS

November 18 - 24

1984

CAPRICORN dec 22 - jan 19	SUN 18	MON 19	TUE 20	WED 21	THU 22	FRI 23	SAT 24
	1A	1B	1A	1B	1BB	1A	1A
	2B	2A	2A	2A	2B	2X	2B
	3A	3B	3A	3B	3BB	3B	3A

AQUARIUS jan 20 - feb 19	SUN 18	MON 19	TUE 20	WED 21	THU 22	FRI 23	SAT 24
	1B	1A	1A	1A	1B	1X	1B
	2B	2B	2A	2A	2BB	2BB	2A
	3A	3B	3A	3B	3BB	3B	3A

PISCES feb 20 - mar 20	SUN 18	MON 19	TUE 20	WED 21	THU 22	FRI 23	SAT 24
	1A	1B	1B	1B	1A	1A	1B
	2A	2B	2B	2A	2AA	2A	2B
	3B	3B	3B	3A	3AA	3A	3B

ARIES mar 21 - apr 19	SUN 18	MON 19	TUE 20	WED 21	THU 22	FRI 23	SAT 24
	1B	1B	1A	1A	1A	1B	1B
	2A	2A	2A	2A	2B	2B	2B
	3B	3B	3A	3A	3B	3A	3A

TAURUS apr 20 - may 20	SUN 18	MON 19	TUE 20	WED 21	THU 22	FRI 23	SAT 24
	1A	1B	1B	1AA	1A	1A	1A
	2A	2B	2B	2AA	2A	2A	2B
	3A	3B	3A	3W	3A	3A	3A

GEMINI may 21 - jun 20	SUN 18	MON 19	TUE 20	WED 21	THU 22	FRI 23	SAT 24
	1B	1A	1B	1A	1BB	1B	1B
	2A	2B	2B	2A	2BB	2A	2B
	3A	3B	3A	3B	3BB	3A	3B

YOUR LUCKY STARS

November 18 - 24

1984

	SUN 18	MON 19	TUE 20	WED 21	THU 22	FRI 23	SAT 24
CANCER Jun 21 - Jul 22	1 B 2 B 3 A	1 A 2 A 3 A	1 A 2 A 3 B	1 B 2 BB 3 B	1 B 2 B 3 B	1 B 2 A 3 A	1 A 2 B 3 A
LEO Jul 23 - Aug 22	1 A 2 B 3 B	1 B 2 B 3 A	1 A 2 AA 3 W	1 AA 2 A 3 A	1 A 2 A 3 A	1 A 2 B 3 B	1 B 2 A 3 A
VIRGO Aug 23 - Sep 22	1 A 2 A 3 A	1 A 2 A 3 A	1 B 2 B 3 B	1 B 2 A 3 A	1 B 2 A 3 A	1 A 2 B 3 B	1 B 2 B 3 A
LIBRA Sep 23 - Oct 22	1 B 2 A 3 B	1 B 2 B 3 A	1 A 2 B 3 B	1 B 2 A 3 A	1 A 2 A 3 B	1 B 2 A 3 A	1 A 2 B 3 B
SCORPIO Oct 23 - Nov 22	1 B 2 B 3 A	1 A 2 A 3 B	1 A 2 A 3 B	1 B 2 B 3 B	1 BB 2 BB 3 B	1 B 2 A 3 A	1 A 2 A 3 A
SAGITTARIUS Nov 23 - Dec 21	1 A 2 A 3 B	1 B 2 A 3 A	1 A 2 A 3 B	1 B 2 B 3 B	1 A 2 A 3 B	1 B 2 A 3 A	1 A 2 A 3 B

105

YOUR LUCKY STARS

November 25 - December 1

1984

	SUN 25	MON 26	TUE 27	WED 28	THU 29	FRI 30	SAT 1
CAPRICORN Dec 22 - Jan 19	1 A 2 B 3 B	1 B 2 B 3 A	1 A 2 A 3 A	1 B 2 B 3 A	1 A 2 A 3 B	1 B 2 B 3 A	1 A 2 A 3 B
AQUARIUS Jan 20 - Feb 19	1 B 2 B 3 A	1 B 2 B 3 B	1 B 2 A 3 A	1 A 2 B 3 B	1 B 2 B 3 A	1 A 2 W 3 AA	1 AA 2 AA 3 A
PISCES Feb 20 - Mar 20	1 B 2 B 3 B	1 B 2 B 3 B	1 B 2 BB 3 BB	1 X 2 X 3 B	1 B 2 B 3 A	1 A 2 A 3 A	1 A 2 B 3 A
ARIES Mar 21 - Apr 19	1 B 2 A 3 B	1 B 2 A 3 A	1 A 2 A 3 A	1 A 2 B 3 B	1 A 2 A 3 B	1 B 2 B 3 A	1 A 2 A 3 A
TAURUS Apr 20 - May 20	1 A 2 A 3 B	1 B 2 B 3 A	1 A 2 A 3 A	1 B 2 B 3 A	1 B 2 BB 3 BB	1 B 2 A 3 A	1 A 2 A 3 B
GEMINI May 21 - Jun 20	1 A 2 W 3 AA	1 AA 2 A 3 A	1 A 2 B 3 B	1 B 2 B 3 B	1 A 2 A 3 A	1 A 2 A 3 B	1 B 2 B 3 BB

your Lucky Stars

November 25 – December 1

1984

	SUN 25	MON 26	TUE 27	WED 28	THU 29	FRI 30	SAT 1
CANCER Jun 21 - Jul 22	1A 2A 3B	1B 2B 3B	1A 2A 3A	1AA 2A 3A	1A 2A 3B	1B 2B 3B	1B 2A 3A
LEO Jul 23 - Aug 22	1A 2B 3A	1A 2A 3A	1A 2B 3B	1B 2B 3B	1BB 2B 3B	1A 2A 3B	1B 2B 3A
VIRGO Aug 23 - Sep 22	1B 2A 3A	1A 2B 3B	1A 2B 3B	1B 2B 3B	1B 2A 3A	1A 2A 3A	1AA 2W 3A
LIBRA Sep 23 - Oct 22	1B 2B 3A	1B 2X 3X	1BB 2BB 3BB	1B 2B 3B	1B 2A 3A	1A 2A 3B	1B 2A 3B
SCORPIO Oct 23 - Nov 22	1B 2B 3A	1A 2A 3B	1B 2B 3B	1B 2A 3A	1A 2A 3A	1A 2A 3A	1A 2B 3B
SAGITTARIUS Nov 23 - Dec 21	1B 2A 3B	1B 2A 3AA	1AA 2A 3A	1A 2B 3B	1B 2B 3B	1B 2A 3A	1A 2A 3B

YOUR LUCKY STARS

December 2 - 8

1984

CAPRICORN dec 22 - jan 19	SUN 2	MON 3	TUE 4	WED 5	THU 6	FRI 7	SAT 8
	1 B	1 A	1 B	1 AA	1 A	1 B	1 B
	2 B	2 A	2 A	2 A	2 B	2 B	2 A
	3 A	3 B	3 AA	3 A	3 B	3 B	3 A

AQUARIUS jan 20 - feb 19	SUN 2	MON 3	TUE 4	WED 5	THU 6	FRI 7	SAT 8
	1 B	1 W	1 A	1 B	1 B	1 BB	1 A
	2 A	2 AA	2 A	2 B	2 B	2 B	2 A
	3 A	3 A	3 A	3 B	3 B	3 A	3 B

PISCES feb 20 - mar 20	SUN 2	MON 3	TUE 4	WED 5	THU 6	FRI 7	SAT 8
	1 A	1 A	1 A	1 BB	1 B	1 X	1 B
	2 A	2 A	2 A	2 BB	2 B	2 B	2 A
	3 B	3 A	3 B	3 B	3 B	3 B	3 A

ARIES mar 21 - apr 19	SUN 2	MON 3	TUE 4	WED 5	THU 6	FRI 7	SAT 8
	1 B	1 B	1 A	1 B	1 B	1 BB	1 B
	2 A	2 B	2 A	2 B	2 B	2 X	2 B
	3 B	3 B	3 A	3 B	3 BB	3 X	3 B

TAURUS apr 20 - may 20	SUN 2	MON 3	TUE 4	WED 5	THU 6	FRI 7	SAT 8
	1 A	1 B	1 A	1 A	1 A	1 B	1 A
	2 B	2 B	2 A	2 AA	2 B	2 B	2 B
	3 B	3 A	3 AA	3 A	3 B	3 A	3 B

GEMINI may 21 - jun 20	SUN 2	MON 3	TUE 4	WED 5	THU 6	FRI 7	SAT 8
	1 B	1 A	1 B	1 A	1 B	1 A	1 B
	2 B	2 A	2 A	2 A	2 A	2 B	2 B
	3 B	3 B	3 A	3 B	3 A	3 B	3 B

YOUR LUCKY STARS

December 2 - 8

1984

	SUN 2	MON 3	TUE 4	WED 5	THU 6	FRI 7	SAT 8
CANCER Jun 21 - Jul 22	1 A	1B	1A	1B	1B	1B	1A
	2 A	2B	2B	2B	2B	2A	2A
	3 B	3A	3B	3B	3B	3A	3A
LEO Jul 23 - Aug 22	1 B	1AA	1A	1B	1A	1B	1A
	2 B	2A	2A	2A	2B	2B	2B
	3 A	3A	3B	3A	3B	3A	3B
VIRGO Aug 23 - Sep 22	1 A	1A	1B	1A	1B	1B	1B
	2 AA	2A	2A	2A	2B	2A	2A
	3 A	3B	3A	3A	3B	3B	3B
LIBRA Sep 23 - Oct 22	1 B	1A	1B	1B	1A	1A	1B
	2 A	2B	2A	2B	2A	2B	2B
	3 A	3B	3B	3A	3A	3B	3A
SCORPIO Oct 23 - Nov 22	1 A	1A	1B	1A	1A	1B	1B
	2 B	2B	2B	2A	2B	2B	2A
	3 B	3B	3A	3A	3B	3B	3A
SAGITTARIUS Nov 23 - Dec 21	1 A	1A	1A	1A	1A	1A	1B
	2 A	2B	2A	2AA	2W	2A	2B
	3 A	3B	3A	3A	3A	3B	3A

your lucky stars

December 9 – 15
1984

CAPRICORN
DEC 22 - JAN 19

	SUN 9	MON 10	TUE 11	WED 12	THU 13	FRI 14	SAT 15
1	B	A	B	A	A	A	A
2	A	B	B	B	A	A	B
3	A	B	A	A	A	A	B

AQUARIUS
JAN 20 - FEB 19

	SUN 9	MON 10	TUE 11	WED 12	THU 13	FRI 14	SAT 15
1	A	A	B	B	B	A	A
2	B	A	B	B	B	A	AA
3	A	A	B	A	B	A	AA

PISCES
FEB 20 - MAR 20

	SUN 9	MON 10	TUE 11	WED 12	THU 13	FRI 14	SAT 15
1	A	B	A	W	A	B	A
2	B	B	A	A	A	B	B
3	B	A	AA	AA	B	B	B

ARIES
MAR 21 - APR 19

	SUN 9	MON 10	TUE 11	WED 12	THU 13	FRI 14	SAT 15
1	A	B	A	B	B	A	A
2	A	B	A	B	B	A	B
3	B	A	A	B	A	A	B

TAURUS
APR 20 - MAY 20

	SUN 9	MON 10	TUE 11	WED 12	THU 13	FRI 14	SAT 15
1	A	AA	A	A	B	A	B
2	W	A	A	B	A	B	A
3	W	A	AA	B	A	B	A

GEMINI
MAY 21 - JUN 20

	SUN 9	MON 10	TUE 11	WED 12	THU 13	FRI 14	SAT 15
1	B	B	B	A	A	A	B
2	A	B	B	B	A	A	B
3	A	A	B	B	A	A	A

110

your lucky stars

December 9 - 15
1984

CANCER Jun 21 - Jul 22	SUN 9	MON 10	TUE 11	WED 12	THU 13	FRI 14	SAT 15
1	A	1B	1B	1A	1A	1B	1A
2	A	2A	2B	2AA	2B	2A	2A
3	B	3A	3A	3AA	3B	3A	3AA

LEO Jul 23 - Aug 22	SUN 9	MON 10	TUE 11	WED 12	THU 13	FRI 14	SAT 15
1	B	1A	1A	1AA	1A	1B	1B
2	B	2A	2AA	2A	2B	2B	2B
3	A	3A	3AA	3A	3B	3B	3A

VIRGO Aug 23 - Sep 22	SUN 9	MON 10	TUE 11	WED 12	THU 13	FRI 14	SAT 15
1	B	1B	1A	1A	1B	1A	1B
2	A	2B	2B	2BB	2B	2A	2B
3	B	3A	3B	3BB	3A	3A	3A

LIBRA Sep 23 - Oct 22	SUN 9	MON 10	TUE 11	WED 12	THU 13	FRI 14	SAT 15
1	A	1A	1A	1B	1BB	1X	1B
2	A	2AA	2B	2B	2BB	2B	2B
3	A	3AA	3B	3B	3X	3B	3B

SCORPIO Oct 23 - Nov 22	SUN 9	MON 10	TUE 11	WED 12	THU 13	FRI 14	SAT 15
1	A	1A	1A	1B	1A	1AA	1A
2	B	2A	2A	2BB	2A	2A	2A
3	B	3A	3B	3B	3AA	3A	3A

SAGITTARIUS Nov 23 - Dec 21	SUN 9	MON 10	TUE 11	WED 12	THU 13	FRI 14	SAT 15
1	B	1A	1B	1A	1AA	1A	1B
2	A	2A	2BB	2A	2AA	2A	2B
3	A	3A	3B	3AA	3A	3B	3B

your lucky stars

December 16 - 22
1984

CAPRICORN Dec. 22 - Jan 19	SUN 16	MON 17	TUE 18	WED 19	THU 20	FRI 21	SAT 22
	1 A	1 A	1 B	1 A	1 A	1 B	1 B
	2 B	2 B	2 B	2 A	2 A	2 B	2 B
	3 B	3 B	3 A	3 A	3 B	3 B	3 A

AQUARIUS Jan 20 - Feb 19	SUN 16	MON 17	TUE 18	WED 19	THU 20	FRI 21	SAT 22
	1 A	1 A	1 B	1 B	1 BB	1 A	1 A
	2 A	2 B	2 B	2 BB	2 B	2 A	2 B
	3 A	3 B	3 B	3 BB	3 A	3 A	3 B

PISCES Feb 20 - Mar 20	SUN 16	MON 17	TUE 18	WED 19	THU 20	FRI 21	SAT 22
	1 B	1 A	1 AA	1 A	1 B	1 A	1 B
	2 A	2 A	2 A	2 B	2 B	2 B	2 A
	3 A	3 A	3 A	3 B	3 A	3 B	3 A

ARIES Mar 21 - Apr 19	SUN 16	MON 17	TUE 18	WED 19	THU 20	FRI 21	SAT 22
	1 B	1 B	1 B	1 A	1 B	1 A	1 A
	2 BB	2 B	2 B	2 A	2 B	2 A	2 AA
	3 BB	3 B	3 B	3 B	3 B	3 A	3 AA

TAURUS Apr 20 - May 20	SUN 16	MON 17	TUE 18	WED 19	THU 20	FRI 21	SAT 22
	1 AA	1 A	1 A	1 BB	1 A	1 A	1 B
	2 A	2 A	2 B	2 B	2 A	2 B	2 B
	3 A	3 A	3 BB	3 B	3 A	3 B	3 B

GEMINI May 21 - Jun 20	SUN 16	MON 17	TUE 18	WED 19	THU 20	FRI 21	SAT 22
	1 A	1 B	1 A	1 A	1 AA	1 A	1 A
	2 B	2 B	2 A	2 A	2 AA	2 B	2 A
	3 B	3 B	3 A	3 A	3 A	3 B	3 B

your lucky stars

December 16 - 22

1984

		SUN 16	MON 17	TUE 18	WED 19	THU 20	FRI 21	SAT 22
CANCER Jun 21 - Jul 22		1A	1A	1B	1A	1A	1A	1A
		2B	2A	2B	2A	2A	2B	2A
		3A	3B	3B	3B	3A	3B	3B
		SUN 16	MON 17	TUE 18	WED 19	THU 20	FRI 21	SAT 22
LEO Jul 23 - Aug 22		1B	1A	1B	1B	1A	1B	1B
		2B	2A	2A	2B	2A	2B	2A
		3A	3A	3A	3A	3A	3B	3B
		SUN 16	MON 17	TUE 18	WED 19	THU 20	FRI 21	SAT 22
VIRGO Aug 23 - Sep 22		1B	1A	1BB	1A	1A	1AA	1A
		2A	2A	2BB	2A	2AA	2A	2B
		3A	3B	3B	3A	3A	3W	3B
		SUN 16	MON 17	TUE 18	WED 19	THU 20	FRI 21	SAT 22
LIBRA Sep 23 - Oct 22		1AA	1AA	1A	1B	1B	1B	1B
		2AA	2W	2A	2B	2B	2A	2B
		3AA	3A	3B	3B	3B	3A	3A
		SUN 16	MON 17	TUE 18	WED 19	THU 20	FRI 21	SAT 22
SCORPIO Oct 23 - Nov 22		1A	1B	1A	1BB	1BB	1B	1A
		2B	2B	2B	2X	2BB	2B	2B
		3B	3A	3BB	3BB	3B	3A	3A
		SUN 16	MON 17	TUE 18	WED 19	THU 20	FRI 21	SAT 22
SAGITTARIUS Nov 23 - Dec 21		1B	1A	1B	1B	1B	1A	1A
		2B	2A	2B	2B	2A	2B	2A
		3A	3A	3A	3B	3A	3A	3B

your Lucky Stars

December 23 - 29

1984

CAPRICORN	SUN 23	MON 24	TUE 25	WED 26	THU 27	FRI 28	SAT 29
dec 22 - jan 19	1 A	1 B	1 A	1 A	1 A	1 A	1 A
	2 A	2 BB	2 A	2 A	2 AA	2 A	2 A
	3 B	3 BB	3 A	3 A	3 A	3 AA	3 A

AQUARIUS	SUN 23	MON 24	TUE 25	WED 26	THU 27	FRI 28	SAT 29
jan 20 - feb 19	1 B	1 B	1 A	1 A	1 AA	1 A	1 A
	2 A	2 B	2 B	2 A	2 AA	2 A	2 B
	3 B	3 A	3 B	3 AA	3 W	3 A	3 B

PISCES	SUN 23	MON 24	TUE 25	WED 26	THU 27	FRI 28	SAT 29
feb 20 - mar 20	1 B	1 A	1 AA	1 A	1 B	1 B	1 A
	2 B	2 A	2 AA	2 A	2 B	2 B	2 B
	3 A	3 A	3 A	3 A	3 B	3 A	3 B

ARIES	SUN 23	MON 24	TUE 25	WED 26	THU 27	FRI 28	SAT 29
mar 21 - apr 19	1 B	1 A	1 A	1 B	1 B	1 BB	1 BB
	2 A	2 A	2 A	2 B	2 B	2 X	2 B
	3 A	3 B	3 B	3 B	3 BB	3 X	3 B

TAURUS	SUN 23	MON 24	TUE 25	WED 26	THU 27	FRI 28	SAT 29
apr 20 - may 20	1 A	1 A	1 AA	1 AA	1 A	1 B	1 A
	2 B	2 AA	2 AA	2 A	2 B	2 A	2 A
	3 B	3 AA	3 W	3 A	3 B	3 A	3 A

GEMINI	SUN 23	MON 24	TUE 25	WED 26	THU 27	FRI 28	SAT 29
may 21 - jun 20	1 A	1 A	1 B	1 B	1 A	1 B	1 A
	2 B	2 A	2 B	2 BB	2 A	2 A	2 B
	3 A	3 A	3 B	3 B	3 B	3 A	3 B

YOUR LUCKY STARS
December 23 - 29
1984

CANCER Jun 21 - Jul 22	SUN 23	MON 24	TUE 25	WED 26	THU 27	FRI 28	SAT 29
	1A	1B	1A	1B	1BB	1B	1B
	2A	2A	2A	2B	2X	2B	2A
	3B	3A	3A	3BB	3BB	3B	3B

LEO Jul 23 - Aug 22	SUN 23	MON 24	TUE 25	WED 26	THU 27	FRI 28	SAT 29
	1B	1A	1B	1B	1A	1A	1AA
	2B	2B	2B	2B	2A	2AA	2A
	3A	3B	3B	3A	3A	3W	3A

VIRGO Aug 23 - Sep 22	SUN 23	MON 24	TUE 25	WED 26	THU 27	FRI 28	SAT 29
	1B	1B	1B	1A	1AA	1A	1A
	2A	2A	2B	2A	2B	2AA	2B
	3B	3A	3A	3AA	3B	3A	3B

LIBRA Sep 23 - Oct 22	SUN 23	MON 24	TUE 25	WED 26	THU 27	FRI 28	SAT 29
	1A	1A	1A	1B	1B	1B	1A
	2B	2AA	2B	2B	2BB	2A	2A
	3B	3W	3B	3B	3BB	3A	3A

SCORPIO Oct 23 - Nov 22	SUN 23	MON 24	TUE 25	WED 26	THU 27	FRI 28	SAT 29
	1B	1B	1AA	1B	1A	1A	1B
	2B	2A	2A	2B	2B	2A	2A
	3B	3A	3A	3B	3B	3B	3B

SAGITTARIUS Nov 23 - Dec 21	SUN 23	MON 24	TUE 25	WED 26	THU 27	FRI 28	SAT 29
	1B	1A	1A	1A	1B	1A	1B
	2A	2A	2A	2A	2B	2A	2B
	3A	3A	3A	3A	3A	3A	3A

YOUR LUCKY STARS

December 30 - 31

1984

CAPRICORN DEC 22 - JAN 19	SUN 30	MON 31	TUE	WED	THU	FRI	SAT
	1A 2A 3B	1 A 2 A 3 B	1 2 3	1 2 3	1 2 3	1 2 3	1 2 3

AQUARIUS JAN 20 - FEB 19	SUN 30	MON 31	TUE	WED	THU	FRI	SAT
	1A 2B 3A	1 A 2 B 3 B	1 2 3	1 2 3	1 2 3	1 2 3	1 2 3

PISCES FEB 20 - MAR 20	SUN 30	MON 31	TUE	WED	THU	FRI	SAT
	1A 2A 3A	1 A 2 A 3 A	1 2 3	1 2 3	1 2 3	1 2 3	1 2 3

ARIES MAR 21 - APR 19	SUN 30	MON 31	TUE	WED	THU	FRI	SAT
	1B 2B 3A	1 A 2 B 3 B	1 2 3	1 2 3	1 2 3	1 2 3	1 2 3

TAURUS APR 20 - MAY 20	SUN 30	MON 31	TUE	WED	THU	FRI	SAT
	1 A 2 B 3 B	1 A 2 A 3 B	1 2 3	1 2 3	1 2 3	1 2 3	1 2 3

GEMINI MAY 21 - JUN 20	SUN 30	MON 31	TUE	WED	THU	FRI	SAT
	1 B 2 B 3 B	1 B 2 B 3 A	1 2 3	1 2 3	1 2 3	1 2 3	1 2 3

your lucky stars

December 30 - 31

1984

CANCER Jun 21 - Jul 22	SUN 30	MON 31	TUE	WED	THU	FRI	SAT
	1 A 2 A 3 B	1 B 2 B 3 A	1 2 3	1 2 3	1 2 3	1 2 3	1 2 3

LEO Jul 23 - Aug 22	SUN 30	MON 31	TUE	WED	THU	FRI	SAT
	1 B 2 B 3 B	1 A 2 AA 3 AA	1 2 3	1 2 3	1 2 3	1 2 3	1 2 3

VIRGO Aug 23 - Sep 22	SUN 30	MON 31	TUE	WED	THU	FRI	SAT
	1 A 2 B 3 B	1 A 2 B 3 B	1 2 3	1 2 3	1 2 3	1 2 3	1 2 3

LIBRA Sep 23 - Oct 22	SUN 30	MON 31	TUE	WED	THU	FRI	SAT
	1 B 2 B 3 A	1 A 2 A 3 B	1 2 3	1 2 3	1 2 3	1 2 3	1 2 3

SCORPIO Oct, 23 - Nov 22	SUN 30	MON 31	TUE	WED	THU	FRI	SAT
	1 A 2 A 3 A	1 B 2 B 3 A	1 2 3	1 2 3	1 2 3	1 2 3	1 2 3

SAGITTARIUS Nov 23 - Dec 21	SUN 30	MON 31	TUE	WED	THU	FRI	SAT
	1 B 2 A 3 A	1 B 2 B 3 B	1 2 3	1 2 3	1 2 3	1 2 3	1 2 3

117

PREFERRED CUSTOMER ORDER BLANK

To: WINICORP
P.O. Box 3314
San Leandro, CA 94578

Reserve me a copy of the 1985 edition of
YOUR LUCKY STARS. By entering the order
before August 1, 1984, I will receive the
new edition for $5.95 + tax and handling.
There will be no increase in price. If
there should be a downward adjustment, I
will obtain the lower price. I under-
stand I will be billed 11/15/84.

NAME:_____

ADDRESS:_____

CITY:_____

STATE:_____ ZIP:_____

P.S. YLS makes a great gift. You may buy
     as many as you choose at your
     preferred customer rate. Write
     number of books desired in box.